Replacing Worry
for
Wonder

Replacing Worry
for
Wonder

A Woman's Secret
to Letting Faith Flourish

Cheri Fuller

An Imprint of Barbour Publishing, Inc.

Print ISBN 978-1-63058-370-5

eBook Editions:
Adobe Digital Edition (.epub) 978-1-63409-182-4
Kindle and MobiPocket Edition (.prc) 978-1-63409-183-1

The author is represented by and this book is published in association with the literary agency of WordServe Literary Group Ltd., www.wordserveliterary.com.

Published by goTandem, an imprint of Barbour Publishing, Inc., P.O. Box 719, Uhrichsville, Ohio 44683, www.barbourbooks.com

Our mission is to publish and distribute inspirational products offering exceptional value and biblical encouragement to the masses.

Member of the
Evangelical Christian
Publishers Association

Printed in the United States of America.

Contents

*For a Discussion and Journaling Guide,
log on to www.gotandembooks.com. This free supplemental
resource is ideal for individual and small-group use.*

STARTING POINT:

What? Me Worried?

*A day of worry
is more exhausting
than a week of worry.*

JOHN LUBBOCK

Has anyone ever said to you, "You look worried!" or "Why do you seem so anxious?" Maybe you've tried to look really calm, or said, "Oh, I'm just concerned." However, there are telltale clues—can you relate to any of these?

You know you're experiencing worry or anxiety when. . .

- The hand rest on the passenger side has permanent imprints from your fingers gripping it for dear life while your teen or spouse drives.
- Your dentist suggests you wear a mouth guard while you sleep because your teeth are grinding down.

- You're giving a speech but can't tell whether the sound you hear is the audience applauding or your knees knocking.
- The words your kids hear most from you when they go out the door is, "Be careful!"
- You have a tape playing over and over in your mind rehearsing all the "what-ifs."
- You discover your nightgown's on backward and your fingernails have become your favorite bedtime snack.

Perhaps you're not wearing a mouth guard *yet*, but have you ever been so worried you couldn't sleep? Or in the face of a difficult or scary situation, your hands have trembled or you've become nauseous? Maybe, like me, you've even struggled with chronic worry, anxiety, or fear since childhood.

We live in an uncertain time where headlines can bring us to a state of mild worry or sheer panic. Terrorist attacks, the epidemic of school shootings, natural disasters like tornados and hurricanes, child kidnappings, and the financial crash of 2007 and 2008 that rippled throughout the United States and globally have caused worry and anxiety to escalate: *Will my child be abducted like all the other children I've read about in the news? Is her school safe? Will I lose my home in a tornado or my job in the next economic recession?*

Even the mention of the words *anxiety*, *fear*, and *worry* have increased in the news, tripling in the early twenty-first century years. And all the way back to September 11, 2001, Americans have been under a blanket of insecurity. Though the magnitude of anxiety began to dissipate with time, many months after the tragedy, thousands reported still having trouble sleeping and making decisions, and pharmacists reported increased demand for antianxiety drugs. Ten percent of travelers either canceled or considered canceling air travel (which may sound small but represents nineteen million airline passengers), and 37 percent at one time or another say they are worried about a biological or chemical attack. Not in a long time have we had so much to be worried or fearful about.

I am no stranger to the worry trap. I know what it's like for my heart to experience terror when I began hemorrhaging in the sixth month of pregnancy or when we rushed our wheezing little son to the emergency room when he couldn't breathe, when four houses in our neighborhood were robbed in one week and I was all alone until my husband returned from military training, and when a loved one got a diagnosis of cancer and a sentence of only a few months to live. But being a worrier didn't start in adulthood.

I came into this world preprogrammed for fretting, and the circumstances of life reinforced it. I was a happy, active, talkative child who loved people, loved to have fun and be outside. But I became more and more cautious as I grew. My dear, protective, and fearful mom tried to keep six children well and safe (one of her sources of pride was getting us all through childhood with no broken bones):

"Don't climb that tree; you might fall!"

"I can't take you kids to the zoo; you might get eaten by one of the animals."

"Don't swim in the deep part of the pool [after we'd had swimming lessons]; you might drown!"

Then a series of devastating losses reinforced that the world was indeed a very scary, out-of-control place: when I was eight years old, my father had his first major heart attack and two more in the next two years. Nine months later, my grandfather died of cancer. When I was ten, my aunt drowned in a tragic accident. And when I was eleven, we woke up one morning to hear that Papa had died in the middle of the night, leaving my mom a thirty-six-year-old grieving, very anxious single parent with six children to raise.

And then less than two years later, after we had moved and I'd started a new school, made friends, and things had begun to restabilize in our family, one of my best friends, just my age of thirteen, died in a hunting accident at his grandpa's farm.

Any vestige of trust or faith I had was blown out of my life with that blast. By my teen years I was afraid of driving on rainy or icy streets and afraid of flying. I worried about change and especially about losing someone I loved. However, since opposites do attract, I married a man who wasn't afraid of much of anything and thrived on adventure. He chose jumping out of airplanes and then tending to the wounded as his number one choice of service in the Air National Guard during the Vietnam War, which gave me something new to worry about.

I don't know what you do when you're afraid, but one of my coping mechanisms is staying very busy, unconsciously trying to not to think about what awful things might happen. Sometimes we can seem to avoid our fears by keeping a frantic pace—being a supermom, wife, soccer mom or dad, or being driven to achieve in our business. Yet underneath we begin to feel more distant from God and see Him as a taskmaster instead of a loving Father.

Scores of people deal with fear by denying it, by sinking into depression and withdrawing from everyone, by abusing alcohol or trying to control things. None of these strategies truly helps us overcome our fears or brings freedom. Instead we can take a close look at what pushes our panic buttons, face our worries, look to God and what He has to show us about what to do when we feel overwhelmed, and find a new freedom and joy in living.

In the pages ahead I'll share with you how God turned my worry into wonder and led me into living the adventure of following Christ.

But this is not just my story. You'll also read true stories of people who were freed from the worry trap. In the first part of the book, after looking at the toll worry takes in our lives, I will share overarching principles that help us overcome worry, fear, or anxiety, such as being centered on who God is, focusing on His truth, the five Ps of Philippians 4, how acceptance makes a difference, and how to pour your energies into prayer instead of ruminating about your worries.

Then beginning with chapter 6, we'll look at how to overcome *specific worries*: worry about your children, about money, about your job or failing to meet everyone's expectations, personal health problems, and crises. Each chapter contains stories for inspiration, strategies for overcoming worry, scriptures and inspirational quotes, and prayers for you to personalize and make your own.

For a free Questions for Discussion guide, log on to www.gotandembooks.com. You can use this guide in a small group or during your personal journaling time, or even in your neighborhood bible study.

How to Get the Most from This Book

What are the worries that weigh you down on a regular basis? What are the situations that push your panic button? The chapters that follow can help move from worry to wonder, help you break free to experience greater faith and peace. Here are some things you can do to get the most from this book:

Keep a notebook or journal handy. You'll need it for specific activities and applications suggested throughout the book. Record questions, memories, and insights that arise as you read. Writing a letter to God in your notebook after a chapter is also helpful. Psalm 62:8 says, "Pour out your hearts to Him, for God is our refuge" (NIV). Besides the fact that pouring out the contents of your heart on paper is one of the best stress reducers, it helps you get in touch with what you're feeling, what God is saying, and how He's working in your life.

Get a package of three-by-five-inch cards to use in some of the chapter applications like making a Peace Packet (which you'll read about), and to record verses that are meaningful to you. Note the "Worry Buster" verses in chapters 2–8, which are excellent for pondering, praying back to God, and memorizing. As you replace negative, fretful thoughts with God's promises and truth, your life will be transformed.

If you'd like to use this book for group or individual study, access the "Questions for Discussion and Reflection" at www.gotandembooks.com and look up the scriptures for going deeper and meditating on God's Word. The questions and study are especially designed to provide opportunities for interaction, discussion, and for applying the material to your real, walking-around everyday life. You can discuss them with a friend, a small group, or sister. Worry and anxiety are good issues to tackle in a group setting, and the support you can offer each other is invaluable.

My prayer is that through reading this book, God will bring you from worry to wonder, and from anxiety to peace. That you'll realize more and more how much God loves you and experience a more joyful relationship with Him.

1.

The High Cost of Worry

Worry does not empty tomorrow of its sorrow;
it empties today of its strength.
CORRIE TEN BOOM

Margot wasn't a big worrier until she found out that in six days she and her kids would be without a home because their landlord had sold their house. Mary Ann's panic button was pushed when a gun and backpack full of ammunition was taken away from one of her daughter's classmates at middle school. Carrie's battle with worry began when her husband was diagnosed with Parkinson's disease and laid off from his job.

Worry is a feeling of concern or anxiety. The word derives from the Old English word *wyrgan*, meaning *strangle*. As we will see, that's what worry can do to us: strangle the very life, energy, and peace out of us. In Middle English the original sense of the verb gave rise to the meaning "seize by the throat and tear," and later *to harass* and *be anxious*.[1]

Anxiety is defined as a fearful concern and apprehension, but it's also a protective emotion that keeps us away from danger and threats to life and limb. These three terms, *worry*, *anxiety*, and *fear*, are strongly related, because chronic or intense worry leads to anxiety. If the anxiety is left uncontrolled, it can develop into full-blown panic or paralyzing fear.[2]

Although men struggle with their share of worries, especially about career and finances, women are

50 percent more likely to be chronic worriers or suffer from anxiety disorders.[3] Women worry about money, personal relationships, appearance, weight, and aging. They worry about children (the number one worry after a woman has her first child), health problems, family, and especially about the future. And the tendency to worry isn't just a condition of the aged. Studies show that worry, anxiety, and excessive stress is increasing rapidly in young adults aged eighteen to twenty-five,[4] and this generation of children takes more antianxiety medication than any in history.

Many people worry about how much they worry. Because it's so common to worry about worrying, psychologists now have coined a new term, *metaworry!*[5]

Mothers especially have a lot to worry about: They worry about putting their kids on the school bus after another school shooting happens across the country. A big worry is that their children will be bullied. Moms fret over germs, especially with all the new strains of superbugs resistant to antibiotics. They worry about their children's health and how they're doing in school. Other moms fear for their kids in the chaotic world they're growing up in.

Single moms are prone to worry about whether

they can make enough money to support their kids. Working moms worry that they're not balancing job and family well enough, about being a good enough mom, not spending enough time with each child, and how they're going to get everything done. A big struggle I've heard from many moms is letting go of control. *If I don't control things, who will? Will everything fall apart?* they wonder. Mothers of adolescents often are afraid their kids may get involved in alcohol, drugs, or the wrong crowd.

Health concerns such as cancer, especially breast cancer, are prominent among things women worry about. If we don't take hormones, we may have heart disease or osteoporosis, doctors tell us, but when the new studies linking breast cancer to estrogen come out, we're afraid if we take them, we're doomed. We try to eat good food, but then the research study of the month shows something we're eating is harmful.

Interestingly, in the realm of the body parts women worry most about as they age, it's not wrinkles or even gray hair, but about how their hands are aging. In the youth-oriented culture we live in, many women fear aging so much, they try to stave it off with Botox injections, plastic surgery, and other cosmetic procedures.

Worry has a negative effect on women in their careers. If they are seen as worriers, women are viewed as indecisive and lacking in leadership skills, and thus passed over for promotions. Some women even fear success because of the role conflict it causes with their mates and their priorities as mothers. Others fear that they can't make it financially on their own if their marriages fail or their husbands are laid off. Single women tell me, "If I lose my job, I have no one to depend on." Or "I'm afraid I'll lose my friend. I continually fear loneliness."

People worry about the unknown, the future, and disasters. Overall, most people's greatest worry is loss: loss of loved ones, loss of health, spouse, or family members. Women today also have a greater fear of violent acts such as rape, robbery, carjacking, and school or workplace violence. As the world grows more uncertain and violent, worry is escalating.

THE EFFECTS OF WORRY

What a toll worry takes in our lives! First, it has a *negative effect on our health*. Studies show that worry decreases our immune system and thus our ability to fight off illness. Chronic worry causes high levels of the stress hormone cortisol in our bodies, which is linked to heart disease and stroke.[6]

Worrisome thoughts cause confusion. Our brains contain more than two billion megabytes of capacity to handle the challenges and problems of daily life. But when we're preoccupied with worry and fear, thoughts become tangled and logical thinking can actually be blocked. Chronically worried people complain they can't concentrate and are easily distracted from daily chores and tasks.

Worry saps our energy. All of us have a certain supply of emotional and physical energy for every day. Yet, if we use it up worrying, we can run out of gas and burn out. We spin our wheels but don't get anywhere. I don't know about you, but I need all the energy I can muster to deal with what's on my plate each day!

Each of us has God-given talents and gifts to bless others with, but *fear and worry keep those talents in the closet.* It causes us to avoid new situations and miss taking advantage of opportunities to develop and utilize our gifts. I love this quote because it's so true: "All of us have reservoirs of full potential," says Swiss psychiatrist Paul Tournier, "but the road that leads to those reservoirs is guarded by the dragon of fear,"[7] a dragon that can sideline you from the very purpose you're designed for, especially when what God is calling you to do involves taking a risk or leaving your comfort zone.

Worry hijacks relationships. Commonsense caution is a good thing, but excessive worry interferes with personal relationships, especially in marriage, with children, and with family members.

Worry sets us up for failure. "I was afraid that was going to happen!" said a mother of a teenage driver who had just had his first wreck. Fear creates what we fear; it has a magnetism that attracts or quickens the approach of the feared event. As Job said, "What I fear comes upon me, and what I dread befalls me" (Job 3:25 NASB). For example, if you're afraid of a dog biting you, you increase the possibility of it happening. If you focus on your fear of gaining weight, you are setting yourself up for extra poundage.

Worry robs us of faith. Just like a seesaw, worry and trust rise and fall proportionately. When one increases, the other decreases.

Worry steals our joy. If you're a visual person with an active imagination, you may turn your anxieties into mental movies that play on the movie screen of your mind. Or you may replay your mental tape recorder with negative messages and what-ifs. In either case, it's hard to be happy and worried at the same time.

All the above are great reasons not to stuff or deny our worries, but to deal with them head-on and break free.

WORRY TO WONDER

In the midst of our anxious, worry-prone world, God tells us throughout scripture, *more than 366 times*, don't be worried, anxious, afraid, or terrified. The One who knows the end from the beginning also knows every emotion men and women will struggle with. Although the fearsome things on this earth seem to multiply, no matter what we have to face, God's message doesn't change:

> *Now the Lord who created you. . .says, Don't be afraid, for I have ransomed you; I have called you by name; you are mine. When you go through deep waters and great trouble, I will be with you. When you go through rivers of difficulty, you will not drown! When you walk through the fire of oppression, you will not be burned up—the flames will not consume you. For I am the Lord your God, Your Savior, the Holy One of Israel. . . .*

*You are precious to me and honored, and I love
you. Don't be afraid, for I am with you.*
(ISAIAH 43:1–5 TLB)

*"Have I not commanded you? Be strong and
courageous! Do not tremble or be dismayed, for
the LORD your God is with you wherever you go."*
(JOSHUA 1:9 NASB)

*"Peace I leave with you; My peace I give to you;
not as the world gives, do I give to you. Let not
your heart be troubled, nor let it be fearful."*
(JOHN 14:27 NASB)

*"Do not fear, for I am with you; do not anxiously
look about you, for I am your God. I will strengthen
you, surely I will help you, surely I will uphold you
with my righteous right hand."*
(ISAIAH 41:10 NASB)

Since God tells us not to be afraid or worried, He must
have some secrets for us. In the next chapter we will
look at the first and most important key: focusing on
the God who can calm our hearts instead of focusing
on our problems, our fears, and the what-ifs.

2.

Centered on the Greatness of God

When we are lost in the greatness of God, we realize that there is no physical, emotional, or social loss so great that God cannot bring good out of it and compensate us in the next life.

GARY THOMAS[1]

It was the dead of winter, and we were living in Yarmouth, Maine. Discouragement was trying to wrap itself around my neck like ivy twining around a house—ivy growing so thick that if left untamed could cover the brick and windows and shut out the light. A cold blanket of worry covered me, draining me of energy. I felt tired, anxious, and burdened.

My husband, Holmes, was out of work and depressed. Day after day he interviewed for jobs and got rejections. Our savings were long gone. I was afraid we couldn't pay the mounting bills. Some days I was worried that Holmes was going to give up; he seemed to have lost hope in life. He was afraid we'd never have the money to return to our home in Oklahoma since there seemed no way financially.

The long-term effects of stress and worry were taking their toll. Normally optimistic and able to encourage my somewhat melancholy spouse, I was struggling. I kept reading my Bible and talking to God in this wilderness season, but my eyes kept landing on the worrisome circumstances. I poured out my heart to Him but heard no answers.

Finally one night I shared with the people in our Monday night Bible study group how trying a time it was for us. Although they prayed for us, things only got worse financially and my worries multiplied. A few weeks later one of the women took me aside and said, "Cheri, no matter how hard things are, you must praise and thank God in the midst of your circumstances. Focus on Him, not your troubles. That's not a message from me but from my missionary friend Anne. She wants you to know she's praying for you."

Are you kidding? I wanted to say. *Thank and praise God when I feel so worried and down about things?* I'd heard Linda talk about this elderly missionary woman who'd served in China before World War II and survived a cruel Japanese prison camp, but I had never met her. I knew she was right and it is what the Bible said, but it was a harsh message to hear in that particular moment. *I always thought You wanted genuine, not fake praise, Lord, and I want to be real with You. How can I rejoice in You and not drown in the circumstances we're in?*

I pondered that question all week, trying to force or will myself to praise God, but I failed miserably. I wanted to be faithful in this but felt overwhelmed by my feelings and drained from trying to bolster my depressed husband. Falling deeper in discouragement and as anxious as ever, I asked Linda the next week if

I could go with her on her weekly trip to see Anne. I thought if anyone could shed some light on my problems, maybe this wise missionary could.

Driving along that bitter cold December day, we saw Anne and her Scottish nurse, Netta's, apartment on the top of the hill. As we walked in, I saw a white-haired woman in a burgundy sweater lying in a recliner, legs propped up and covered with a small green blanket. Print house shoes peeked out from the blanket.

Above the old missionary hung a plaque with the words LET US EXALT THE LORD TOGETHER. Another said, JESUS FIRST. A humidifier hummed. After taking our coats, Netta and Linda went into the other room to wrap Christmas packages for mailing to missionaries they supported. Although they had very little financially, they regularly gave to missionaries and were remembering each with a scripture calendar this year.

TRUST GOD

Anne was almost totally blind, but her spiritual eyesight blew me away. She spoke with effort but a quiet authoring, asking me all about our situation. She seemed to have an understanding of my life far beyond what I shared. After listening, she began to offer some insights: "For your children's and your husband's sakes, you must praise and thank God and show in your countenance your faith in Him. For she who trusts Him finds Him wholly true.

"Trust and thank God in all things," she continued. "Praise Him even if tears are running down your cheeks."

I nodded but grimaced inside, thinking this sounded impossible. "But how?" I asked. "I want so much to praise and thank God, and I've tried, but it's so hard when I'm worried and depressed."

"By trusting God implicitly," she added. "You can't depend on your feelings; they are Satan's playground. Ask for God's grace to praise Him and He'll give it to you."

A few moments later, Linda and Netta came in with our coats and began to bundle Anne up to leave for the restaurant. As painstakingly slow and difficult as it was with her diabetic condition and leg problems, Anne needed to get out once a day and walk with her walker, so back into the cold we went. Linda and I walked on each side of the elderly woman, our arms under hers.

> To adore God means we love Him with all the powers within us. We love Him with fear and wonder and yearning and awe.
>
> —A.W. Tozer

A STORY OF GOD'S FAITHFULNESS

Over our salads and bowls of soup, I asked Anne about her experiences as a missionary in China. She shared about the day she was leaving Shanghai for furlough in her beloved Scotland. After nine years of service with the China Inland Mission, she couldn't wait to see her family and friends and was overdue for a respite. She and the other missionaries had packed their belongings and stepped out of the mission house to get on the boat when Anne heard a clamor outside. As she watched through the window, she saw Japanese soldiers goose-stepping in unison down the street, knees almost up to their noses. The Lord spoke to her heart, *"Anne, come aside. I want to talk to you."*

Reminding her of His care and provision during many adventures and close calls, He told her she was not going home but would be a prisoner of the Japanese. He didn't tell her how long, but she distinctly heard, *"I'll be with you."* A precious, very real sense of God's nearness and peace filled her as He spoke. Then, *"Do you have any prayer requests to make, Anne?"* He asked.

Although she'd never given her teeth a thought, the Spirit nudged Anne to pray that her teeth would be preserved and not one of them fall out. So out of obedience more than vanity, she asked this of God.

Moments later she and the other English and American missionaries were taken prisoner and marched to a Japanese prison camp. There she spent three and a half years in near starvation, dreadful cold in winter, scorching heat in summer. Cruelty, rats, disease, and death were all around her. There were no Bibles, so she had to rely on all the verses she'd committed to memory.

She chuckled as she told me about the rat she'd found up her sleeve in the middle of the night and the "rat patrol" she headed up after that to try to make the barracks a safer place for the other women and children. She shared about God's constant presence, of the people who came to know Christ, how she gave Him every burden, worry, and fear and saw Him work time after time. Anne seemed to possess this quiet assurance that she could absolutely trust God because He was worthy. She could have been overwhelmed by worry or consumed by despair until she couldn't minister at all, but she didn't focus on the what-ifs: *What if I don't survive? What if my health breaks? What if we're not rescued?*

Instead, she fixed her eyes on Jesus and His promise that He would never leave, fail, or forsake her (Hebrews

13:5–6). He hadn't failed her yet in her years on the mission field, and she knew she could count on Him for tomorrow. So she used her energies instead to serve God, to proclaim Christ, and love those around her.

As she related stories about God's provision in the prison camp. I sat there spellbound, marveling at the mercy and faithfulness of God. And as I listened, our trials came into perspective in the light of these experiences.

Anne was released after World War II ended. And although in poor health, every tooth was preserved. But other losses awaited her. Her mother had died while she was in prison camp. And although now she was dealing with the day-to-day trials of aging, her vision failing, and she'd suffered several surgeries, she encouraged my

> Relinquishment of burdens and fears begins where adoration and worship of God become the occupation of the soul.
>
> —Frances J. Roberts

friend and me: "Trust. Cast all your cares and worries on Him. No matter what's on your mind, roll it onto His shoulders and rest under His wing."

On the way home, my thoughts were filled with what Anne had said. It was as if she had pulled my eyes off the problems and fixed them on Jesus. Her words came back to me: *"Don't lean on your own understanding. Don't trust what you see or feel or think; trust God and His Word. He's faithful even when we're not."*

I prayed silently, "Lord, I want to focus on You and praise You right in the middle of our circumstances, and I ask for Your grace to do that."

THE TURNAROUND

That night the checking account balance hadn't changed. My husband still didn't have a job and was just as withdrawn and depressed as usual, but something new was engaging my thoughts. The next few days in the early hours before the kids got up, I searched the Bible, especially the Psalms, for words to praise God, to center my thoughts on Him. All the feelings of worry and anxiety were still lurking around, trying to drag me down, but I knelt and used these verses to adore the Lord. This time I didn't wait until I felt better.

As I did, that deep heaviness began to lift and with it the worry about the stack of unpaid bills. It was as if dark glasses were removed and I saw what I'd never seen before: that no matter how difficult or trying our situation was, and even if nothing external changed, I could praise and thank God because the trial would only draw me into a closer relationship with Him.

Like a trickle from a frozen creek in the spring, the icy, troubled thoughts within me began to thaw little by little, and thanksgiving bubbled up. Slowly at first, my perspective began to change. I wasn't a prisoner of my feelings but could trust and enjoy God for the first time in a long time—no list of complaints or requests. I thanked Him for the inner work He was doing in us, for our health, our children, our marriage that was still together, and how even the fact that it was strained had drawn me closer to depend on Him for the plan He had for us even though we hadn't seen it, even for the financial losses because they reminded me of the temporariness of material things and our eternal treasures in Christ.

LOST IN THE GREATNESS OF GOD

How could Anne face what she did and not be overcome by fear or despair? She was centered on God, lost in His greatness, focused on His faithfulness, love, and character. Whatever worries you have, whether related to finances, children, health, or anything difficult you face, focusing on God is a key to overcoming worry when life gets precarious.

"Keep looking in the right direction in everything you do—that is so important. Keep looking up and kneeling down," said Corrie ten Boom, another woman who overcame the horrors of a German concentration camp and took the message of Christ's love and forgiveness around the world following her release. One day she met a missionary who was desperate because Christians were continually being killed near her home.

"Look down on the storms and terrible events around us, down from on high," Corrie told her, "from the heavenly realms where Jesus' victory is the greatest reality. This is only possible by the Holy Spirit." She told the woman how she and her sister Betsie were walking around the prison grounds at 4:30 a.m. when God performed a miracle. Betsie would say something, Corrie would say something— then the Lord would speak, and they both heard Him at the same time. "I cannot explain it, but it was wonderful. We saw then that even though everything was terrible, we could rely on the fact that God did not have any problems, *only plans*. There is never panic in heaven! You can only hold

> The larger the God we know, the larger will be our faith. The secret of power in our lives is to know God and expect great things from him.
>
> —A.B. Simpson

on to that reality through faith because it seemed then as it often seems now, as if the devil is the victor. But God is faithful, and His plans never fail! He knows the future! He knows the way."[2]

That vision of God's greatness empowered Corrie to not worry or panic even though she faced overwhelming loss, pain, and danger, and it sustained and strengthened her when she traveled the world in her sixties and seventies to share the message He gave her. Just as God was for Anne, Corrie, and countless believers throughout history, He will be our stability in an unstable world. He is our unchangeable certainty when everything around us is changing. And there's no more secure, safe place than in the center of His will and purpose for our lives.

Having our eyes on the Lord in this way is vital—David experienced it and described it throughout the Psalms. No matter how bad he was hurting or what he was fearing, he turned his focus to God and proclaimed who He was. Though he was surrounded by a host of enemies time after time, he could say, "The LORD is my light and my salvation—whom shall I fear? The LORD is the stronghold of my life—of whom shall I be afraid?" (Psalm 27:1 NIV). Paul, too, said we must fix our eyes on Jesus and press on to know Him (Philippians 3). Even John, the great disciple, needed to have his eyes on the Lord (Revelation 1).

When we look to God and focus on Him instead of our problems and worries, we gain His perspective and our distress begins to subside. It doesn't mean we won't go through difficult times or experience pain. But we begin to know and believe that we can trust Him in the midst of our circumstances, for He is trustworthy.

WORRY TO WONDER

Our faith as believers isn't just a passport to heaven; eternal life doesn't just start when we die. It begins here on earth as we make Jesus the center of our lives. The importance of knowing God and focusing on Him is described in John 17:3: "This is eternal life: that they know you, the only true God, and Jesus Christ, whom you have sent" (NIV). How can we stop being preoccupied by our worries and problems and get lost in the greatness of God?

Cultivate a lifestyle of praise. Why did Anne encourage me to praise and thank God even when I didn't feel like it? Because it gets our eyes off the mountains to the mountain mover. It has many other benefits as well.

We're not talking about praise as just a few worship songs sung at the beginning of a service, but a God-ward focus in the midst of whatever we're facing. It's realizing as Ruth Myers, a missionary with the Navigators since 1972, said, "God uses tough situations to draw you nearer to Him and to enrich your praise."[3]

This doesn't mean denying your real feelings. You may be experiencing intense feelings of fear or sorrow. It's expressing your distressing emotions (including worry, despair, guilt, fear, or anger) to God—yet choosing to keep proclaiming who He is and turning to Him in spite of how things look—and not postponing this until you feel better. It's moving *toward the Lord* instead of *away from Him* in your distress and developing a faith that goes beyond your feelings.

> The remarkable thing about fearing God is that when you fear God you fear nothing else, whereas if you do not fear God you fear everything else.
>
> —Oswald Chambers

At first you may start to thank God with little trickles as I did, but if you persist, even in the darkest of places, you will find those trickles of faith will turn into a fountain. Your attitude can turn from anxiety to trust. You may even begin to see your situation differently: "Praise can heighten your awareness that distressing circumstances are God's blessings in disguise. Your trials rip away the flimsy fabric of your self-sufficiency. This makes room for God's Spirit to weave into your life a true and solid confidence—the kind of confidence that Paul expressed in Philippians 4:13: 'I can do all things through Christ who strengthens me' (NKJV)."[4]

When we focus on God and proclaim who He is, we begin to see clearly who's in control. Our focus is drawn from the complexity of the problem to the adequacy of God's infinite resources.[5]

Fear God instead of people or circumstances. The Bible tells us to exchange a fear of situations or persons for a fear of God. A holy, healthy fear comes out of reverence, awe, and wonder of the God who created us, knew us before we were even born, and loves us. David demonstrated the fear of God many times. When he faced formidable enemies, "he understood that he could not simply will his fears away. The person (or persons) he feared had to be displaced by something bigger: *fear of the Lord and trust in His provision*," says Dave Shive.[6] It's choosing a vertical focus, a wonder and awe of God instead of a horizontal focus on our circumstances, people, or problems.

Know His name. I'm convinced that our puny or incorrect perspective of God is the root of many of our most distressing emotions. And I know when I let worries—over finances, the future, health, or anything else—sap my strength, it's because I've forgotten how awesome, how able, how loving and faithful God truly is.

"Those who know your name trust in you, for you, Lord, have never forsaken those who seek you," says Psalm 9:10 (NIV). Our faith in God develops as we know His names. As I have lived together with my husband Holmes for thirty-three years, I've come to know him in the different aspects of his nature as my companion, best friend, prayer partner, generous giver, father of our children, and now also, grandfather, builder of beautiful homes, and much more. In a similar way, we know God in experiencing different aspects of His character and person—or what in the Bible is known as "his names," through the ways He revealed Himself in the Bible.

> The larger the God we know, the larger will be our faith. The secret of power in our lives is to know God and expect great things from him.
>
> —A.B. Simpson

Thus I've found that when I become anxious or

fearful about things, one of the best antidotes is to re-focus on God by meditating on His names, that He is Elohim, Creator of the whole universe, yet He cares about me and my family. That He is Jehovah-Nissi, the Lord My Banner, and His banner over me is love. One of God's names is Emmanuel, God with us—not at a distance, but nearer than our breath, constantly work-ing in our lives. His name is Jehovah-Rapha, the Lord Our Healer, who specializes in healing relationships and broken hearts and renewing our weary spirits. In reminding myself of who God is and getting Him more clearly into focus, my heart becomes centered on God and finds courage to trust Him once again.

When I understand more about God's nature, my heart begins to trust Him. And coming to Him with my needs or the needs of others in prayer is a whole dif-ferent matter than just hoping that He might help me. It's *knowing whom we're addressing*, it's being confident that we aren't asking anything outside of who God is. For example, we can trust that we can pray to Jehovah-Jireh, the Lord Our Provider, He sees our needs and delights to provide for them because that is who He is. Just as He provided in the past, He'll provide in the fu-ture. That is who He is, and it's an essential part of His nature He wants us to experience. The more we know Him, the more our faith grows, and the more our worry turns to wonder about what a great God we serve.

WORRY BUSTERS

Praying scripture is one of the most powerful things we can do to dissolve our worries and grow in our relationship with the Lord. In the next chapter, we're going to delve into focusing on God's Word, praying scripture, and exchanging the lies for the truth. And in each chapter there will be verses for you to pray back to God. To begin, take one of the following verses and let the prayer below it be a springboard for your own communication with God:

> *O magnify the LORD with me,*
> *And let us exalt His name together.*
> *I sought the LORD, and He answered me,*
> *And delivered me from all my fears.*
> *They looked to Him and were radiant,*
> *And their faces shall never be ashamed.*
> (PSALM 34:3–5 NASB)

—∞—

Lord, I want to magnify You and exalt Your name. I am seeking You and asking that You would deliver me from all my fears. As I look to You, I thank and praise You that You've promised I will be radiant and my face shall never be ashamed.

—∞—

Why are you in despair, O my soul?
And why have you become disturbed within me?
Hope in God, for I shall again praise Him
For the help of His presence.
(PSALM 42:5 NASB)

—◠—

Praise him in his Temple, and in the heavens
he made with mighty power. Praise him for his
mighty works. Praise his unequaled greatness. . . .
Let everything alive give praises to the Lord! You
praise him!
(PSALM 150:1–2, 6 TLB)

—◠—

Father, I admit that I've been in despair and fear, my heart disturbed within me. I want to hope in You, for with the help of Your presence and Your Spirit, I will again praise You! I praise You for Your mighty power and mighty works!

3.

Focusing on the Truth

Just as saving faith comes through hearing the gospel, so also the faith to trust God in adversity comes through the Word of God alone. Only in scripture do we find an adequate view of God's relationship to and involvement in our painful circumstances. Only from the scriptures, applied to our hearts by the Holy Spirit, do we receive the grace to trust God when we are afraid.

JERRY BRIDGES

When Cathy's daughter Susan was going blind, she agonized over what was happening. Susan had a car in the driveway she couldn't drive, her boyfriend dropped her suddenly, and her college roommate moved out the week before finals without saying a word, leaving her alone the last eight weeks of the spring semester. Susan's family had prayed with and for her, trusting God with the situation. But their struggles continued with a vengeance as her blindness progressed rapidly that summer.

As a mother, Cathy had never gone through an experience as painful and worrisome as this one. She would sleep at night but upon awakening, tears would already be streaming from her eyes. Worried thoughts would rush in. . . . *Will Susan be able to finish college? What about her dreams? What about marriage and her future? Who will marry her if she's blind?* She cried and then washed her face and picked up her Bible and began to candidly talk to God.

> Oh, that we would turn eye and heart from everything else and fix them upon this God who hears prayer until the magnificence of His promises and His power and His purpose of love overwhelmed us!
>
> —Andrew Murray

"Lord, You know I've taught women in Sunday school for years that You are my comfort and hope; I feel nothing but sadness. I need Your comfort just now." As she read, verse after verse soothed her aching heart and strengthened her to face the day and minister to her hurting daughter, her family, and the women in her Sunday school class.

Each morning as Cathy read the Bible, God gave her a different verse of His hope, His security, and comfort. From this, she learned she must let Christ set her heart mood for the day from His Word and focus on what God said instead of what she felt. If she looked at worrisome circumstances or why something happened, she'd spiral downward to depression and fear.

> All the promises in the Bible become your property. But you have to find your way around in that world of riches. You have to find out how rich you are.
>
> —Corrie ten Boom

One morning when she read Isaiah 26:3, "He will keep in perfect peace all those who trust in him, whose thoughts turn often to the Lord" (TLB), Cathy had an idea: to write these verses to carry with her everywhere she went to focus her mind on throughout the day. As she did, she found not only did it keep her from dwelling on the dismal what-ifs, but her thoughts were gradually transformed from worry and sadness to a confident sense of peace.

Charles Stanley once said, "The most valuable item you can own in the time of trouble is a Bible." Cathy found hers indispensable. The Word of God was alive and powerful as she learned not to keep her attention riveted on a constant rehearsal of what had happened to her daughter or all the whys, for that would make her easy prey for Satan—but on the truth. Day by day with her "Peace Packet," as her collection of Bible verses in a small ziplock bag came to be known, she focused on Christ and His promises.

Verses such as "I am with you and will rescue you" (Jeremiah 1:8 NIV) and "Jehovah himself is caring for you!" (Psalm 121:5 TLB) dispelled fear. Psalm 112:6–9 became a passage that strengthened her faith: "For the righteous will never be moved; he will be remembered forever. He is not afraid of bad news; his heart is firm, trusting in the LORD. His heart is steady; he will not be afraid, until he looks in triumph on his adversaries, He has distributed freely; he has given to the poor; his righteousness endures forever; his horn is exalted in honor" (ESV).

As the summer went by, Cathy began to type up these verses on cards because women in her class were going through their own trials and they asked for them. As they noticed what peace, comfort, and strength came, her collection grew and so did the demand for it. The little Peace Packet that came from one family's grief has been used to help many more: a man whose wife was critically ill, a young woman whose husband left her with two children, a missionary in harm's way in South America, a family in the emergency room awaiting word on their teenager who'd been in an auto accident.

To share the rest of the story: though Susan's vision did continue to deteriorate, she finished college, even traveling to Finland on a student exchange program. She pursued many of her dreams and married. She, her husband, and their son run a horse ranch in a western state, and God has truly done more than she could have asked, thought, or imagined. It doesn't mean this one experience was the end of their suffering. But over and over Cathy has seen that God's promises are as fresh and real and glorious to them today as they were in their darkness over twenty years ago.

THE LIFELINE OF GOD'S WORD

Every time we open our Bibles, we encounter the

Living Word, verses which are God-breathed truths meant to break us free from worry, from fear, and anything else that would hold us in bondage (John 8:32). His truth brings us out of old patterns of worried, anxious thinking and helps us fight the good fight. We certainly can't fight these powerful emotions in our own strength, wish them away, or hope they will go away if we think positive thoughts.

BREAKING FREE

Grace's world changed suddenly at age eight when she was sexually assaulted by two distant relatives at a family reunion. Threatened with harm to her and her family, she kept silent, and the emotional devastation continued into her adult life. She was so afraid of people that she withdrew and spent most of her time alone. She didn't get too close to any males, worried the abuse would happen again. She was distrustful of God, and she didn't even trust herself. She eventually surrendered all hope of knowing freedom or joy again.

> Faith is like radar that sees through the fog—
> The reality of things at a distance that the human eye cannot see.
> —Corrie ten Boom

Yet Grace continued to be a seeker. She wanted so

badly to break through the walls that kept her isolated and afraid. One morning she was reading in John 11 of Lazarus's resurrection. Jesus called to Lazarus to *come out.* Then He told observers to take off Lazarus's grave clothes (vv. 43–44). In that moment, God spoke to her heart: *"Grace,* come out. *Let others take the grave clothes. Be free."* She wept that morning as she knew that God was asking her to trust others to help her. For the first time ever she told someone—her best friend—what had happened, and they wept together. Her friend's compassion freed her to experience God's love and acceptance and allow others into her life.

Realizing how bound she was, she asked God to send someone to help her take steps toward freedom. Soon after, she met a lay counselor at church. As she shared her life story, the friend began to lead Grace through Romans and Psalm 18. She taught her biblical truth about her position in Christ and the power of the cross in daily living. God's Word became a light in her darkness as she learned to stand on its authority.

One by one, she confronted the lies she'd believed about God, herself, and others with biblical truth and started seeing changes. Although she knew nights would be scary, she decided she could live alone. She could travel alone for business if necessary and even be out after dark. She didn't have to use being overweight as her armor anymore. She could trust people's intentions toward her, reclaim her voice, and stop being a people pleaser.

John 10:10 says, "The thief comes only to steal and kill and destroy" (NIV), but Jesus came that we "may have life, and have it to the full." Worry and sadness had stolen years of Grace's life, but God's promises gave her the courage to wage war against it. Finding a counselor and asking others to pray for her helped her come to a new level of freedom. Grace still struggles

> How firm a foundation,
> ye saints of the Lord,
> Is laid for your faith in His
> excellent Word!
> What more can He say
> than to you he hath said,
> To you who for refuge to
> Jesus has fled?
> — *How Firm a Foundation*,
> words from "K" in Rippon's
> Selection, 1787

with fear and weight, but she's resolved not to allow it to hold her down. It takes effort on her part to choose, believe, and live out biblical truth. But even when she struggles, she is confident that:

> *The LORD is my rock, my fortress and my deliverer;*
> *my God is my rock, in whom I take refuge,*

> *my shield and the horn of my salvation,*
> *my stronghold.* (PSALM 18:2 NIV)

With such a God and such powerful truth, fear cannot overcome her.

One of the best things Grace learned to do is to replace the worried thoughts that kept her up at night with truth she was learning as she grew in Christ, like these:

If you're suddenly diagnosed with an illness and a wave of fear and anxiety floods your mind, thoughts like you'll never be able to work again and support yourself or your kids with the limitations you'll face, that you're so weak you don't know how you'll cope, or that this illness slipped by God's watchful care, it is vital to focus on the Word.

Instead of letting those troubling thoughts roll through your mind, believe and meditate on the truths: that God will supply all you need (Philippians 4:19); and regardless of the health issues, you are strong in Him (Joel 3:10); and He has given you all you need for life and godliness (2 Peter 1:3). That He is your Great Physician, Jehovah-Rapha, the God Who Heals, and is well able to take care of your physical needs (Exodus

15). That you belong to Christ (1 Corinthians 3:23) and nothing happens apart from His affectionate, watchful care of you (1 Peter 5:7).

As you displace your worries with God's Word, you will be filled with a new confidence and hope. As you read through specific worries in the chapters ahead, you'll find scriptural truths that relate to them.

WORRY TO WONDER

We need a bridge to move from living a worried life to walking in trust and peace, and we don't have to invent one. God already provided it in the Bible. Here are some ways to apply it to your life:

Empty the backpack of burdens. What are you most worried about? What concerns keep you awake at night? Be specific by saying, "I'm so worried about _____" or "I'm so burdened about _____, and _____, and _____."

You may need the help of a counselor or trusted friend you can talk honestly with and gain insight into what is really troubling you. Once you admit instead of deny what you are most afraid of, the light can begin to shine there. Roots begin to be revealed and recovery can begin.

Stand on the promises. Once you've begun to face your worries and confess them to God and another person, study the Bible to discover God's precious promises that address those issues. His Word is indestructible and irresistible, enabling us to trust in the dark, even in the most uncertain places and trials.

That's why it's so important to renew your mind day by day with God's Word (Romans 12:2) and look for specific truths to replace the faulty thoughts you previously have ruminated on.

A truth like "I am able to do all things through Him who strengthens me" (Philippians 4:13 HCSB) replaces the thought, *I just can't handle this situation. It's too hard!* Replace the thought that there's nothing good ahead for you, that you've failed and life is over with the great promise in Jeremiah 29:11–13: "For I know the plans I have for you, says the Lord. They are plans for good and not for evil, to give you a future and a hope. In those days when you pray, I will listen. You will find me when you seek me, if you look for me in earnest" (TLB).

And when you feel like nobody cares about you, fill your heart with these verses: "How precious to me are your thoughts, God! How vast is the sum of them! Were I to count them, they would outnumber the grains of sand" (Psalm 139:17–18 NIV).

Make a Peace Packet. A great way to integrate these truths into daily life in a practical way is to create a Peace Packet. It will help you apply truth to your life and will remind you we have a loving God who'll be faithful to fulfill His promises. Whether your worries relate to your job, your child, your safety, or the future, God's Word applies to *you* and your situation. Here are some suggestions for making and using your own Peace Packet:

- On a three-by-five-inch card, bright colored if you prefer, write out a verse that has encouraged you or speaks to your situation or worry.
- Repeat the promise in your own words, telling God you are depending on Him. For example, "God, You said You would lift the fallen and those bent beneath their loads, that You are close to all who call on You sincerely (Psalm 145:14–21). Now I trust You to do this in my life."
- Put the cards in a small ziplock bag to carry with you wherever you go.

- Focus on these truths instead of your worries; read them in the morning, before you go to sleep, and in in-between moments.
- Add to the verses in your Peace Packet as you discover more. Ask God each day to show you a new truth; it's a prayer He loves to answer.
- Give the verses away by sharing them with others who need an encouraging word. Then they truly become your own. *Pray God's Word.*

When we pray the promises, we become filled with faith instead of fear and doubt. That's why you'll find scripture prayers throughout this book. As we do, we can trust God to fulfill them in His way and time.

> It is by prayer that we couple the powers of heaven to our helplessness, the powers which can turn water into wine and remove mountains in our own life and in the lives of others.
> —Ole Hallesby

"The more we incorporate the scriptures into our praying, the more likely we are to pray in the will of God, for God always stands behind what He has said. . . . When we let the Bible become our prayer, we are praying an inspired vocabulary. It will often release deep inner feelings far better than extemporized prayers that will come from our minds," says Judson Cornwall.[1] Psalm 138:2–3 confirms it: "I will bow down toward your holy temple and will praise your name for your unfailing love and your faithfulness, for you have so exalted your solemn decree that it surpasses your fame. When I called, you answered me; you greatly emboldened me" (NIV).

WORRY BUSTERS

Who shall separate us from the love of Christ? Shall trouble or hardship or persecution or famine or nakedness or danger or sword? . . . No, in all things we are more than conquerors through him who loved us. For I am convinced that neither death nor life, neither angels nor demons, neither the present nor the future, nor any powers, neither height nor depth, nor anything else in all creation, will be able to separate us from the love of God that is in Christ Jesus our Lord. (ROMANS 8:35–39 NIV)

—∞—

Lord, I thank You that nothing can separate me from Your love in Christ Jesus. Nothing—trouble, hardship, danger, death, or any powers or force, now or in the future—can remove me from Your hand. How I praise You for Your forever love that holds me. Give me a steadfast heart to believe and confidently stand on this truth, whatever I face in my life.

—❦—

Fear not; stand still (firm, confident, undismayed) and see the salvation of the Lord which He will work for you today. (EXODUS 14:13 AMP)

—❦—

God, strengthen me by Your Spirit to be confident in You and not to shake in my boots. Empower me to trust You until I see Your salvation worked in my life. As I turn from worry to focus on You, fill me with awe and wonder about how great You are.

4.

From Panic to Peace

The more you pray, the less you'll panic.
The more you worship, the less you worry.
You'll feel more patient and less pressured.
RICK WARREN

Esther helped her elderly patient settle into a bed in the outpatient oncology center where she served as a nurse. She chatted comfortably while gathering supplies and preparing the medication for the patient's chemotherapy.

All her patients were favorites, but this woman held a special place in her heart. Even after twenty years of nursing, Esther still prayed each morning for God to guide her in treating her patients, for protection for their veins and from dangerous side effects. This morning had been no different, and she trusted Him.

> A great many people are trying to make peace, but that has already been done. God has not left it for us to do; all we have to do is to enter into it.
>
> —D. L. Moody

"Let me check your IV site," she said, making sure the needle was securely in the vein. Then she carefully read each page of the chart to be sure she had all the information needed. Since the platelet counts were low, Esther called the oncology doctor to verify treatment. He couldn't be reached, but the nurse in charge assured her the doctor had ordered chemo and two units of blood. Esther turned back to her patient and gently took her hand. Then the medications flowed into her vein.

As the last of the chemo was given, the phone rang. "Whatever you do, *don't* give the patient chemotherapy today. I guess you saw that her counts are too low," said the doctor.

"I already gave her treatment," Esther replied.

"What? How could you be so incompetent?" he screamed. "You'll probably be responsible for this patient's death!"

Suddenly she was struck with a horror that she may have harmed her patient.

When her husband Tim picked Esther up a few hours later to drive to a retreat in a nearby state, her stomach knotted tightly. The doctor's tirade still rang in her ears as she thought, *I'll probably go to jail if this patient dies.* This is the nightmare that every nurse hopes and prays will never happen to her—that *her mistake* could kill a patient.

All the way down to the conference center, Esther was consumed with worry: *God, how can I pray over my patients and trust You and then have this happen?*

If she dies, even if I don't go to jail, I'll lose my nursing license, she thought. *Can I really trust God at all?* Her stomach tightened until she felt as if she'd be sick. *She's so precious. . .not just a patient, but a friend. I couldn't live with myself if I caused anything to happen to her.*

The fear of her patient's dying was overwhelming. Even with her husband's encouraging words, she was overwhelmed by the fear that her patient could die.

By the time they arrived at the conference, Esther was a wreck. Even though it was warm outside, her body felt cold. When she ran into Bill, the speaker and a dear friend, the story poured out: "I may be responsible for a patient's death," Esther cried. "I can't think of anything else. How can I even concentrate on the seminars when my patient may be in danger?"

> Through faith you have become a child of God, you have been saved, and through faith you also achieve victory over worry, fear, and other sins. Cast your burdens on the Lord. You do that when you pray.
>
> —Corrie ten Boom

"I think you're at just the right place. Come to the first session I'm doing on worry and fear," Bill said. After putting their suitcases in the room, Esther reluctantly went to the meeting, doubtful anything he said could quell her fears.

In the first session, Bill explained that he'd always struggled with fear and worry until he discovered the "four Ps" in Philippians 4:6–8: "Be anxious for nothing, but in everything by prayer and supplication with thanksgiving let your requests be made known to God. And the peace of God, which surpasses all comprehension, will guard your hearts and minds in Christ Jesus. Finally, brethren, whatever is true, whatever is honorable, whatever is right, whatever is pure, whatever is lovely. . .if there is any excellence and if anything worthy of praise, dwell on these things" (NASB).

I know these verses by heart, Esther thought. *I don't see how hearing them again can help me. What am I doing here? I may as well go home and face the consequences.*

"You see," Bill explained, "whenever God commands us to do something—in this case, *not to worry or be afraid about anything*—He always follows with *how to do it.* So here's what these verses show us to do:

"The first P is to *pray* about what worries you. Give your worry or burden consciously and specifically to God. Paul's saying in essence, 'Don't have anything to do with anxiety. Stop fearing and start praying!'

"The second P is to *praise* and thank Him for what He will do in the situation. Thank God for the person or situation causing you worry because even this very problem is one more reason to trust Him.

"The third P is to receive God's *peace.* If you've prayed about the problem and given it to God, then He will move in on your mind and heart with peace through Christ Jesus. It's a promise."

As Esther took notes, what the speaker was saying began to make sense. Her thoughts were just as oppressive as when they arrived, but she listened intently as he sketched on the board the remaining P.

"The fourth P is what to do next. Focus your mind on God. Focus on all the *positive*, wonderful things about His character instead of being preoccupied with negative thoughts, how you're going to get out of this mess, or the 'what-ifs.' Center your mind firmly on God's goodness."

Praying the Four Ps

When Esther returned to her room after the seminar, she had a long talk with God. "I've always been able to count on everything in Your Word. I'm going to put these verses into practice, regardless of how I feel," she said. She prayed through the four Ps, mechanically at first, and gave the whole situation and her patient to God. She prayed for God to pour out His tender mercies and healing power in this woman's life and to protect her and bless her. Thanking Him for this awful trial was hard, but when she did, she experienced a few brief minutes of peace.

However, five minutes later, the worries started up

again. Over and over again she gave the problematic situation to God, thanked Him the best she could for how He was working, and consciously focused on His character and truth. Each time, she received a little bit longer respite of peace. As she continued praying this way, those small blocks of peace gradually grew from five minutes to ten and then twenty.

But the next morning when she awoke, Esther's heart was beating wildly. *She's going to die. I'm going to prison. Who will care for Tim and our four girls?* She went against the strong tide of her feelings, got down on her knees, and prayed according to the pattern in Philippians. And this time when the anxiety returned, it wasn't with as much agony.

Throughout the second day and while listening to other messages, she kept giving God her problems, offering her thanks, centering her mind on His faithfulness. The moments without worry grew.

By Sunday, the peace she was experiencing, even before she knew if anything had changed or what news she'd get at the hospital the next day, was so profound, she couldn't make herself worry. Before, when her thoughts wandered to the situation, she was filled with terror. But in those three days of almost continual prayer, she'd moved from despair to confidence in God—whatever the outcome.

Amazingly, in the next few weeks, Esther saw with her own eyes her patient not only improve, but her cancer go into remission. Although the doctor never admitted the final dose of chemo had helped turn her condition around, Esther knew God had been at work in her patient's life as well as her own.

The pattern of prayer in Philippians 4, casting all her cares and worries on God and thanking Him in the midst of struggles, cultivated a deep intimacy that sustained Esther in waves of difficulty and tragedy that hit her life in the next few years: her mother-in-law's massive stroke, which necessitated Esther becoming her full-time caretaker in their home. It kept her from panic during the death of one daughter, the out-of-wedlock pregnancy of another daughter, her husband's cancer and surgery, and their move to another state where God was calling him to pastor.

Instead of panicking, Esther prayed, and found God's incredible peace was always

> Through faith you have become a child of God, you have been saved, and through faith you also achieve victory over worry, fear, and other sins. Cast your burdens on the Lord. You do that when you pray.
>
> —Corrie ten Boom

available. Be anxious for nothing—let nothing worry you—covers a lot of ground. It covers fear, guilt, anger, all the things that cause anxiety to well up.

By handling troubling producing situations with prayer, whether it's a small concern (*I'm afraid this hairdresser is ruining my hair*) or a big one (*I'm afraid my patient is going to die* or *I'm afraid my child is going to leave God and youth group and get into drugs*)—God instead of the circumstances becomes our focus, and peace replaces panic.

Wonder replaces worry—wonder at God's peace, which is more than the human mind can comprehend, wonder at His faithfulness and provision, so that we can "celebrate God all day, every day. . .revel in him!" (Philippians 4:4 MSG).

A. W. Tozer calls this the "astonished wonder" and awe that is at the heart of true worship. This sense of "spiritual astonishment" or wonder happens among men and women when the Holy Spirit is present, working in their lives, just as what happened in Esther's life.

Prayer needs to be our *first resource*, not a last resort as we face problems in daily life. In our stressful world, prayer is the best thing we can do to quiet our hearts and thoughts. Even secular medical research is revealing the amazing effects of prayer. Studies at Duke University and elsewhere show that daily prayer is so effective in reducing stress that it cuts women's risk of anxiety by as much as 81 percent. The act of praying triggers biochemical changes in the brain and adds a sense of safety and purpose to our lives.

CATAPULTED INTO PRAYER

It's an amazing thing that the very things that push our panic buttons can catapult up into earnest prayer. When people discover I write and speak on prayer they ask me, "Have you always been a praying person? Have you always had a passion for prayer?" They think perhaps I was born on a prayer mountain in Korea to parents who were veteran intercessors and that I loved, even as a child, to spend hours alone with God praying.

Oh no! Quite the contrary. I was born into a busy family of six kids in Dallas, Texas, and of all the siblings, I was the most "Martha," the most distracted and busy doing many things. Though I have a sister named Martha, I tended to be more Martha than she was. And even as Mama led us in "Now I lay me down to sleep. . ." every night, I could barely wait for the "Amen" to turn on the flashlight under the covers to read my latest book or roll my hair on pink sponge rollers in the dark.

But God apprehended me and brought me into the school of prayer. He began to develop a "Mary" heart in me alongside my productive Martha tendencies through my concern for my children, as you'll read in a subsequent chapter. I came to the realization that in this broken world there was very little I could control (in fact, control was an illusion), but that my greatest influence for good in my own family and others' lives was *prayer*.

I had a huge love for people and hated to see friends, family, and especially children suffer. My heart broke for them. But the Lord showed me the first, best, and most important thing I could do for them was to *pray for them* (and then through praying, He might show me what practically I could do for them).

Prayer became *my first resource*, not a *last resort* as often we treat it, and He transformed me from a worrier into a warrior—a prayer warrior, that is. The pattern of prayer gradually broke the pattern of worry and fear.

Do I give God my problems and worries all the time and leave them with Him? No, many times I take them back and start fretting again like this little poem "Broken Dreams" expresses:

As children bring their broken toys
With tears for us to mend
I brought my broken dreams to God
Because He was my friend.
But then instead of leaving Him
In peace to work alone,
I hung around and tried to help
With ways that were my own.
At last I snatched them back and cried,
"How can you be so slow?"
"My child," He said, "what could I do?
You never did let go."

—Unknown

That's why we're to *practice*, which is the fifth P. Paul says in Philippians 4:9, "Whatever you have learned or received or heard from me, or seen in me—put it into practice" (i.e., don't do this one time and give up if the worry comes back! Keep practicing!). "And the God of peace will be with you" (NIV).

To *practice* means giving our concerns to God (and give them back if we start obsessing over them again), to *practice* thanking Him in the midst of difficulties because it's another chance for Him to show Himself mighty in our lives, to *practice* receiving His peace and dwelling on the positive instead of the negative.

God wants us to give them all to Him: our shattered dreams, deepest burdens, worries, and pain. He can handle them, transforming our panic into peace and our worry into wonder. It's kind of like pouring out water from a pitcher—we pour out these burdens and problems, which makes room for God to pour in His peace, joy, love. So keep pouring! Keep practicing! Keep praying!

> Through faith you have become a child of God, you have been saved, and through faith you also achieve victory over worry, fear, and other sins. Cast your burdens on the Lord. You do that when you pray.
>
> —Corrie ten Boom

In the simple act of letting go of your fears and problems, you will experience His presence, which is far more wonderful than we can imagine; you will have a changed perspective; you will draw near to God in your difficulty—and He promises to draw near to you (James 4:8).

Worry to Wonder

We each have different "panic buttons" and certain experiences that shake our lives. Sometimes it's a single calamitous event, like the death of a spouse or job loss (or the threat of such a loss). Other times misfortune comes as it did in Job's life—an earthquake of tragedy plus waves of difficulty and pain. But no matter what your particular fear or panic button is, the five Ps will work—not because they are a magic formula. But because when we put God's Word into practice and lay the tracks down in prayer for His power to come, we emerge from darkness into His marvelous light. Here's how to start:

The moment you're struck by anxiety, go right to God. Pull away wherever you are and get into God's presence. That means at work or even in the midst of a conversation—take the worry to Him instead of engaging it in your mind and thinking of all the terrible things that could happen. When something bad happens, we have a tendency to blame God for allowing us to go through the difficulty. Instead, regardless of what the situation is, thank God about how He's blessed you recently and:

- how He's drawing you to Him through this fear or problem
- what He is going to do in the situation
- how you're going to grow
- how God is going to reveal Himself in the need or concern

As you choose to turn to God and praise Him, it delights His heart. All of life tries to pull you down to circumstances but when you focus on the Lord, He blesses you with the ability to cope with the problem.

"Thanksgiving gives effect to prayer," says Robert Jamieson, "and frees us from anxious carefulness by making all God's dealings a matter for praise, not merely for resignation, much less murmuring. Peace is the companion of thanksgiving."[1]

Persist and don't give up. What if you've prayed through the five Ps and given your worry to God and it comes back a few minutes later? Don't give up. Remember that the bigger or heavier the fear or problem, the more times you may need to give it to God until you have really let go of it. If the fear recurs, don't say, "Well, this isn't working." Instead, stop and give your worry to God again. Each time you'll get a little more victory. Peace will increase until your mind is *at rest* concerning the matter. *Rest* means mental and spiritual tranquility, freedom from all worries. And that's often when the creative solution or insight of what you're to do will come to mind—when you're at mental and emotional rest.

> If God be our God, He will give us peace in trouble. When there is a storm without, He will make peace within. The world can create trouble in peace, but God can create peace in trouble.
> —Thomas Watson

Receive His peace. Philippians 4:7 says, "The peace of God, which surpasses all comprehension, will guard your hearts and your minds in Christ Jesus" (NASB). Claiming God's peace is a matter of yielding to Him and receiving what He freely offers. Peace isn't what you conjure up to make yourself feel better about the situation. It's not affirming self-talk, but claiming the peace of God—a peace we can't fathom or measure—that will transform your very thoughts. Christ's whole nature is peace. He is the Prince of Peace.

The Message's translation of that verse says, "Before you know it, a sense of God's wholeness, everything coming together for good, will come and settle you down. It's wonderful what happens when *Christ displaces worry at the center of your life*" (emphasis added). And isn't it amazing that the problem doesn't have to go away for us to experience this peace? Yes, we want it to be resolved; but as soon as it is, another one will take its place. Though we aren't promised a problem-free life, we can trust this promise from God: He will give us the power and peace to live abundantly—even in the midst of adversity.

Pray with others. There's nothing better than to join hearts and hands in prayer with other believers about the things that we are most worried about. God didn't mean for us to be like the Lone Ranger, tackling problems alone. When the battle is fierce or long, we naturally get discouraged and need other friends in Christ to pray with us—and they will need us to lift them up for their concerns, too. Even the great leader Moses needed Aaron and Hur to support him and hold his arms up in prayer as he interceded for the Israelites when they were in battle against the Amalekites (see

> Our Lord, our God, deliver us from the fear of what might happen And give us the grace to enjoy what now is and to keep striving after what ought to be.
>
> —Peter Marshall

Exodus 17). You and I need prayer partners, a group to pray with, or sometimes a whole network of prayer or church-wide intercession in a crisis time. Whether you're young or old, a Mary or a Martha, a man or woman— God is calling all of us to pray about our families' lives and what's going on in the nation and world.

Let prayer become a way of life. The "practice these things" part of the Philippians passage can remind us to pray using the five Ps in the small worries and the larger burdens every day. Prayer opens the door to the One who can save us from our fears and redeem our situation. As you practice prayer, giving your concerns and burdens to God will become as natural as breathing. Just as soldiers in warfare practice the maneuvers and strategies to be ready to use them in real combat, practice these five Ps so you'll be ready when your personal battle comes:

PRAY
PRAISE
PEACE
POSITIVE THOUGHTS
PRACTICE—PRACTICE—PRACTICE

To leave your old habit of worry and start a new habit, write the above words on a card with the words of Philippians 4:6–9. They will remind you every day to release your worries to God in prayer. As you make them a part of your lifestyle, you'll find the five Ds: dread, doubt, depression, despondency, and disease—will disappear. It's in practice that the truth of Philippians 4 will move from your head to your heart, that the joy of the Lord will be the strength you need, not just to survive but to worship God with an astonished sense of wonder and enjoy Him right in the midst of it.

Worry Busters

Humble yourselves, therefore, under God's mighty hand, that he may lift you up in due time. Cast all your anxiety on him because he cares for you.
(1 Peter 5:6–7 NIV)

God, thank You that You invite me to roll everything upon You, casting just like a fisherman casts his line into the lake, all my worries and fears and things that I'm concerned about, because You love me affectionately and care for me. I give You my deepest cares now....

—⁂—

"Peace I leave with you; my peace I give to you. Not as the world gives do I give to you. Let not your hearts be troubled, neither let them be afraid." (JOHN 14:27 ESV)

—⁂—

Jesus, I admit my heart has been troubled and afraid. Help me to choose to turn to You instead of staying agitated and fretting about my problem. You have given Your peace, and I receive it and thank You for it! What a wonderful gift! I don't have to live worried and unsettled, but I can be free to experience Your peace and joy.

5.

Acceptance: The Door to Peace

*This is what the Sovereign LORD, the Holy One
of Israel, says: "In repentance and rest is your
salvation, in quietness and trust is your strength."*
ISAIAH 30:15 NIV

Marilyn was exhausted the morning she and her husband, Dave, came home from his month at the rehab center. Every day she'd handled the load not only of caring for their three children but fielding calls from angry bill collectors, as well as operating car pool, working a part-time job, and trying to run the household by herself. Dave emerged in better shape than he'd been in months; he was happier than he had been in a long time. Marilyn, however, was a wreck.

In her room that morning she cried out to God, "I've prayed for ten years about our finances, and look what's happened." Her tirade continued as she looked over her journal entries and scriptures she'd prayed and clung to in the past year. Seeing the stack of bills she couldn't pay, she sobbed in discouragement, "I just don't believe You anymore!"

> Faith is...
> Letting go of my demands that another change and looking to God for the change He sees I *need*.
>
> —Pamela Reeve

Marilyn was angry at God for all the unanswered prayers, angry at friends who hadn't confronted Dave with his alcoholism sooner, before it wrecked their life, mad at Dave for his addiction, and angry at herself for putting up with the awful situation for so long.

But most of all, she was terrified about what they were going to do now that her mate was sober but out of a job. Worried thoughts constantly plagued her so that she couldn't even sleep at the end of a long day. As Dave passed their bedroom and saw Marilyn on the floor crying, he asked, "What's the matter with you?"

"What's wrong with *me*? Everything! But right now I don't understand these finances and why we can't ever pay our bills. I've trusted God, and He's let me down," Marilyn answered, tears flowing down her cheeks.

"Remember, acceptance is the answer to all your problems," he said, and breezed by on his way to the garage, glibly reiterating a principle he'd learned at the rehab center.

You mean I'm supposed to accept that we don't have any money, that my husband's an alcoholic, that our life has crashed? she thought, continuing to sob. Then as she got quiet and began to think about it, Marilyn realized for the first time her focus was always so fixed on Dave's flaws and financial problems that she'd never accepted *anything*. She'd wanted God to fix everything. But when it didn't happen, she was crushed by disappointment, her mind tangled by worry about what they were going to do.

She was trying to "pray in" those things she wanted and kept looking to the future when her prayers would be answered her way. But it never happened! Marilyn's life was like what C. S. Lewis described in the movie *Shadowlands*: "We live in the Shadowlands. The sun is always shining somewhere else, around the bend in the road, over the brow of a hill." And today, once again, her eyes were fixed right over that hill.

So that day Marilyn pulled out her journal and began to write, "Acceptance is the answer to all my problems today." She wrote down all the problems she faced, all the anxieties she had about them. "Lord, I've prayed, tithed, worked, and nothing has opened up to us. So I know that if You wanted to, You could change things in a moment or a day. But You haven't. So I accept the way things are today, all the things I can't change. I want You to show me what You're doing. I want to see You and trust You, in the here and now right in the midst of our mess."

As Marilyn waited in the quiet, peace slowly began to replace the worry. In the process of writing, she remembered what God had done even in the last few months. The "wilderness blessings" they'd received were many. They were living in a rented house, but it was a large, lovely one, and the owners had allowed them to live there rent-free while Dave was at the rehab center and until they recovered financially. She recalled the friends who'd supported and helped them; the ones who brought meals, the friend who gave her clothes when she had no money to buy any. She also began to see God was doing an inside job, teaching them a deeper level of responsibility and changing them both.

Until now she'd been just like the Israelites complaining about the manna God had provided in the wilderness. While she was looking down the road from the Shadowlands, she'd missed the things God was doing today. Her worry and anger dissipated as acceptance and gratefulness grew.

Two women looked through prison bars
One saw mud, the other saw stars...
Each of us has a choice about how we look at life: We can focus on the mud or lift our eyes and see the stars. Every woman has circumstances that appear to be prison bars. God wants you and me to learn to be content in our circumstances, not when they improve.

—Linda Dillow

As author Hannah Hurnard says, the only way to live victoriously in the midst of life's difficulties is "by learning to accept, day by day, the actual conditions and tests permitted by God, by a continually repeated laying down of our own will and acceptance of His as it is presented to us in the form of the people with whom we have to live and work, and in the things which happen to us. Every acceptance of His will becomes an altar of sacrifice, and every such surrender and abandonment of ourselves to His will is a means of furthering us on the way to the High Places to which He desires to bring every child of His while they are still living on earth."[1]

WHEN EMOTIONS OVERWHELM

From that point to the present, whenever Marilyn begins worrying about a situation, she repeats the process that brings her to acceptance.

No, the circumstances didn't change overnight. But she has learned to walk in a daily peace and rest in God right in the middle of the problems she faces. Getting her journal out, she starts a new page, writing at the top: "Acceptance is the answer to all my problems today."

She lists the needs and problems that worry her the most. Then she thinks of the next right thing she should do and writes it down. On one day she realized she needed to stop charging on her credit cards; on another, to call a financial counselor and ask for help. One day when she asked God what He wanted her to do, it was very practical: *make a budget and live on it*. These were things she *could* change that might make a difference.

Then Marilyn began to journal, writing about the things she *couldn't* change that day. Doing this, she learned that if there was a nagging irritation with a person or situation, it was probably a good indication she wasn't accepting it. For example, when she was constantly irritated that her husband wasn't a sharp dresser and wore things she thought looked tacky, she wasn't accepting him. Or when the rental house they were living in was a continual burr under her saddle, then she wasn't accepting it as God's present provision.

As she listed the issues, it gave her time to think through them: *Can I change it in any way? Have I prayed about it? Could God change it if He wanted to? Have I asked Him to show me my part to do? Is He asking me to do something? Is God listening? Am I listening?*

Then she wrote what God's Word had to say about those matters, noting the verses that came to mind. For example, to address her concern about whether God is listening: "God has surely listened and has heard my prayer. Praise be to God, who has not rejected my prayer or withheld his love from me!" (PSALM 66:19–20 NIV). To address the house she didn't like and was afraid she was going to be stuck in forever: "I have learned to be content in whatever circumstances I am," Paul said, ". . .with humble means" or living in prosperity. . . "of having abundance and suffering need" (Philippians 4:11–12 NASB) and "Godliness with contentment is great gain" (1 Timothy 6:6 NIV).

She used the Psalms to praise God, not to try to manipulate Him to do what she wanted, but to express her love and thankfulness. "True praise is not an attempt to manipulate God into producing the precise results we hope for," says Ruth Myers. "Instead it helps us accept our situation as it is, whether or not He changes it. And if we continue praising God, it helps us reach the place where we can say, 'Father, I don't want You to remove this problem until You've done all You want to do through it, in me and others.' "[2] James 1:4 underscores this thought: "Don't try to get out of anything prematurely. Let it do its work so you become mature and well-developed, not deficient in any way" (MSG).

What Acceptance Is and Isn't

Sometimes we equate "acceptance" with an attitude of "anything goes": *I'll accept any behavior my husband or children dish out.* Instead, acceptance is embracing and dealing with the problem behavior while loving the person. For example, if you discover your son has a drug problem, acceptance is admitting and acknowledging that he has a drug problem. Nonacceptance of that fact is denying his drug use and pretending it doesn't exist. If you're accepting the problem, you are:

- there to get him help, which may involve loving confrontation and arranging for treatment.
- accepting him as a person, but not his inappropriate behavior.
- setting boundaries at home.
- listening to the needs of his heart and praying for him.

All the while, you are loving him unconditionally in that sickness; doing whatever common sense, the Bible, and reliable counsel advise you to do. None of the above includes being a doormat for your son, enabling his behavior and drug abuse to continue.

Acceptance doesn't mean you quit praying and

resign yourself to a negative future; it doesn't mean becoming irresponsible or giving up. While it isn't any of these things, it is realizing that *you can trust God*— trust Him to bring an answer, though perhaps not the answer you'd expected *and* to weave things into a pattern for good even out of the trying situation or problem. It is knowing that when you are tuned in to God and His Word, *and asking Him*, He will show you His part. But if there is nothing you can do to change today's situation, acceptance is trusting God to get you through anything.

Acceptance is facing the storms of life with God's peace, which will bring you into the reality of the *now* (instead of the far-off fantasy) and allow you to see more of what He's doing and what He's called you to today. At the same time, walking in this kind of acceptance and trust in God will drain away worry, fear, and anxiety.

FROM CONTROL TO REST

I've found that the more we worry, the more we try to control people or situations. That causes us to be more fearful, especially when the people we're trying to control resist us or the situation backfires.

How do we get out of this control trap? Fenelon, in his wonderful volume of letters entitled *Let Go*, written in the seventeenth century and yet just as alive and applicable today, captures the spirit of acceptance: "If you recognize the hand of God and make no opposition to His will, you will have peace in the midst of affliction. Happy indeed are they who can bear their sufferings with this simple peace and perfect submission to the will of God."[3]

How can you and I experience this kind of quietness and confidence instead of turmoil and worry in the midst of crisis? How can we face whatever comes with acceptance rather than resignation? A look at the story of Shadrach, Meshach, and Abednego in Daniel 3 gives us insights:

The three young Israelite men were being thrown into the fiery furnace because they refused to bow to the Babylonian idols. They faced a crisis as severe as any we might ever encounter in life. And if God didn't come and deliver them, they would surely die. Here's how they were able to walk through the trial without fear: In addition to all their prayers and worship, they made a commitment:

> *[They replied to the king], "O Nebuchadnezzar,*
> *we do not need to defend ourselves before you in*
> *this matter. If we are thrown into the blazing*
> *furnace, the God we serve is able to deliver us*
> *from it, and he will deliver us from Your Majesty's*
> *hand. But even if he does not, we want you to*
> *know, Your Majesty, that we will not serve your*
> *gods or worship the image of gold you have set*
> *up."* (DANIEL 3:16–18 NIV)

David Wilkerson, once the pastor of the Times Square Church in New York City, concludes that we are always to pray in faith, believing that God will answer, yet trusting Him completely with our situation, saying, "But if not, Lord, *I'm still going to trust You!*"[4]

That's acceptance at its deepest level: knowing Christ Jesus will come into our crisis and walk through it with us. Yielding ourselves to Him and His will and trusting that whatever happens, He's faithful and *He'll never leave us or forsake us.* The peace and freedom from fear that comes with this kind of confidence in God is sufficient for any of our earthly trials.

Worry to Wonder

Acceptance says, "True, this is my situation at the moment. I'll look unblinkingly at the reality of it. But I'll also open my hands to accept whatever a loving Father sends. Thus acceptance never slams the door on hope."[5] Here are some steps to take toward accepting your situation:

Write in your journal the things and people in your life, including their behaviors, you have the hardest time accepting. Take a good, honest look at what you have difficulty accepting.

Then ask, "What are You asking me to do regarding each problem? What do You want me to take action on?" Ask what is *your part*, what is *God's part*, and what is the other person's part, so you don't try to do everyone else's part. Then write what God's Word has to say about each issue. Go to the concordance in your Bible for help in discovering wisdom to apply to these situations. Store up His truth and then talk to Him about it by turning these verses into prayers.

Shift from questioning or demanding of God, "When

> We survive the packages of pain God allows in our lives by remembering who God is and what He has done in the past.
>
> —Linda Dillow

are You going to take this problem away?" to asking Him, "What is it You're shaping in my life through this trial or difficulty? What can I learn from this experience?" Oh, how the Lord is often just waiting for us to ask this so He can show us. A humble, teachable attitude can minimize the frustrations we feel when the trial we're in continues long past when we think it should be over.

This kind of attitude reminds me of what Andrew Murray suggests we say in time of trouble:

> First, The Lord brought me here. It is by His will I am in this strait place; in that will I rest.
> Next, that He will keep me in His love and give me grace in this trial to behave as His child.
> Then, He will make the trial a blessing, teaching me the lessons He means me to learn and working in me the grace He intends for me.
> Last, in His good time He can bring me out again, how and when He knows.[6]

Say I am here, he says: by God's appointment, in God's keeping, under His training, for His time.

I have to admit that in the midst of some of my

own personal trials, this seemed a hard message to hear. But the more I've pondered Murray's advice, I realized that knowing that my situation doesn't take God by surprise and that there *will be a time He brings me through it*, and that He will use it to shape and mold me to be more like Christ, is encouraging after all and helps me to embrace God's will instead of resist and resent it.

Cultivate a sense of humor, a lightheartedness about yourself and your problems. Sometimes this is the hardest thing for us serious folks who are burdened and worried about a circumstance! When we look at ourselves and our issues too seriously, we become difficult to live with and lose perspective. A lively sense of humor helps us accept ourselves and become more accepting of others. It is *good news* that God loves and accepts us in spite of our messes and failures.

Develop a sense of gratitude and wonder about life. As Marilyn did, don't forget to acknowledge to a friend or write down the ways God has given blessings in your wilderness season or trial.

Perhaps because I lost my parents, grandparents, and best friend early in life, I believe that each day is a gift from God we haven't earned or deserved, so there is always something to thank Him for. There's always something to celebrate even if things are difficult: the beauty of a glowing blue and red sunset; an unexpected note your teen who's been giving you trouble left that said, "I love you, Mom," a juicy piece of watermelon on a hot day... Just like the expectant wonder you felt long ago about Christmas, delight in God's blessings, large and small, every day no matter what the difficulties are.

WORRY BUSTERS

And be satisfied with your present [circumstances and with what you have]; for He [God] Himself has said, I will not in any way fail you nor give you up nor leave you without support. [I will] not, [I will] not, [I will] not in any degree leave you helpless nor forsake nor let [you] down (relax My hold on you)! [Assuredly not!] So we take comfort and are encouraged and confidently and boldly say, The Lord is my Helper; I will not be seized with alarm [I will not fear or dread or be terrified]. What can man do to me? (HEBREWS 13:5–6 AMP)

—m—

Lord, grant me Your grace to be satisfied and accepting of my present circumstances and with what I have, knowing that You'll never fail or forsake me, that you will always support me and that You are *for me*. Nothing can happen to me apart from Your loving hand. I take comfort and am encouraged and want to say with confidence, You are my Helper! I will not fear or be terrified!

—∞—

Jesus, I want to know more of Your kindness and peace, but most of all, I want to know *You*! Open my eyes to get a fresh vision of You. Thank You for giving me everything I need, for sharing Your goodness with me. Thank You that by Your power You've given me the rich and wonderful blessings You have promised. How can I not trust You, such a great God that You are!

6.

Overcoming Worries about Our Children

Prayer, even prayer for what God desires, releases
power by the operation of a deep spiritual law;
and to offer up what one loves may release still more.
SHELDON VANAUKEN

Dread tied my stomach in knots before I ever opened my eyes that September Sunday morning. Even in deep sleep I listened for the sound that sparked fear in me. The rattling sound was all the scarier because it emanated from the chest of my six-year-old son, Justin.

His skin was pale and drawn; his chest heaved as he gasped for a breath. I looked into his blue eyes and saw a reflection of my own fears.

Scrambling out of bed, I ran for his inhaler. Asthma had accelerated my worry that had even grown to anxiety. I'd tried so hard to protect my children, giving them nutritious meals and vitamins, hovering over them like a quail with her covey. My husband, Holmes, thought I was being overprotective, and I knew I was. But how could I explain the horrible dread that welled up in me, especially when our firstborn was so sick we had to take him to the emergency room?

When asthma hit Justin at age four, it hadn't been a simple case of wheezing. His first attack had been full-blown *status asthmaticus*, that took days in a hospital to bring his breathing back to normal.

That's what I hated most about asthma—I was powerless to control it. An attack could hit any moment, changing our plans. This chronic illness had stolen my joy and overtaken our life. It had even curtailed our holiday travel to the grandparents' ranch in Texas because we'd surely wind up in a hospital due to the climate change.

Just as we always did, we consulted with the doctor on the phone that day, gave Justin all his medicine, and made sure he used his inhaler and rested. But this time nothing worked. Even with careful nursing, as the day grew longer, his wheezing worsened.

So by 10 p.m. that night, we dropped our two younger children at a neighbor's and sped to the hospital emergency room in the rain. After several injections of adrenaline and IV medications didn't snap him out of the attack, the ER doctor called our pediatrician.

> Through prayer we can open a window to God's love.
>
> —Unknown

When I saw him strike down the long, gray hall, I breathed a sigh of relief. *I just know he can get Justin's asthma attack under control. He always has before.*

"Raise the level of aminophylline and cortisone. Give him another Adrenalin injection," he ordered the ER nurses. "An asthma attack is like a ball rolling down a hill," Dr. Spencer told us in the hall. "We've got to stop it with the biggest guns available before it gets any closer to the bottom. Don't worry—you'll probably be home in a few hours." He turned on his heels and disappeared down the hall.

But at 2 a.m. the nurse called Holmes and me out of the cubicle. "Your son is not responding as well as he should be. We'll have to admit him to the hospital. If you'll just go down the hall to Admitting and sign the papers, we'll get him upstairs to a room."

DASHED HOPES

My spirits fell like the rain pelting the window beside me. Swallowing a huge lump in my throat, I thought about the yellow Snoopy lunch box our son had picked out, the new jeans and red plaid shirt waiting on his bunk bed for the first big day of school. "Holmes, there's no way he'll be well enough to start school!"

"I think we have a lot more to worry about than school," he bristled. After we got our son all settled in his fifth-floor room, Holmes sent me home to stay with Alison and Chris while he kept vigil next to Justin's bedside. I just *knew* he'd be better in the morning.

But when I walked in at 8 a.m., Justin was white faced, an oxygen tube in his nose. The muscles in his neck and chest strained as he fought for air. Every breath sounded like a rib-rattling staccato. In spite of other treatments, his condition worsened throughout the day. On his afternoon rounds, Dr. Spencer examined him again, shook his head, and took us out in the hall.

"Something inside his body has got to rally. We've done everything I know to do," he told us.

Stunned, I couldn't believe what I had heard. My heart raced. The rising anxiety cracked the thin veneer of calm I'd tried so hard to maintain.

"Why don't you go home for a while?" Holmes said.

"I can't leave now."

"You've got to nurse Alison and reassure Chris. They haven't seen you for hours. Besides, you aren't much help unless you pull yourself together. You're only making him nervous," he said.

I hated to leave, but I knew he was right. In a dazed fog, I rode the elevator down and walked out the front door of the hospital. A loud clap of thunder startled me. A slap of cold rain stung my face. I searched up and down the rows of parked cars but couldn't find our station wagon anywhere. Finally, soaked and shivering, I ran back into the hospital to wait for the storm to let up. Huddling next to the door, I noticed the sign: CHAPEL.

Reluctantly, I slipped into the empty chapel and was drawn to the large white Bible at the front, open to Psalm 42:

> *Why, my soul, are you downcast?*
> *Why so disturbed within me?*
> *Put your hope in God, for I will yet praise him,*
> *my Savior and my God.* (v. 5 NIV)

Finally, in the quiet, I prayed, "Lord, I've put my hope in the doctor, the medicine, Holmes, and myself to save our son. That's why I'm in so much despair and fear. I've trusted You in some areas of my life, but I've clung to my kids, trying to keep them safe. I even dedicated them in a church service, but I never really entrusted them totally to Your care. I'm like the disciples who in the midst of a fierce storm, cried out to Jesus, 'Master, Master, we are perishing!'"

And a quiet inner voice said to me as He had to the disciples, *"Cheri, where is your faith? Peace. . .be still."*

Lightning caused the chapel lights to flicker off and on, and thunder boomed outside, turning my thoughts again to God.

The Creator of the whole universe—in complete command of the thunderstorm outside, yet I couldn't trust Him with my son's life. In not releasing him to God's care, it dawned on me that I was thwarting the very power that could help him.

"Hope in Me," I felt Him say. *"Trust his life to Me totally."*

I bowed my head and this time said, "Father, forgive me for not trusting him to Your care sooner. I forgot that he was Your child first and that You made him. I give him to You, whatever happens."

As I walked outside something warm began to melt away those icy feelings that had gripped me. The torrent of rain had turned to a drizzle. After searching several rows in the parking lot, I found our car.

I drove up the hill to get on the expressway. When I slowed at the YIELD sign, I looked up and was struck by a tiny sliver of terrifically bright sunshine that broke through the black clouds.

At that moment, a huge weight lifted inside me and a feeling of peace unlike I'd ever experienced swept through me. Justin was safe and cared for. In some inexplicable way I knew this. . .knew I could trust God with our precious firstborn son.

I spent a happy, unhurried hour with Chris and Alison in our favorite yellow rocking chair at home, munching cheese and crackers and reading Richard Scarry books to them.

An hour and a half later I returned to the hospital and walked into our son's room. He was sitting up in bed, coloring a picture, and chatting with his grandparents who'd just arrived from east Texas. A smile lit up his rosy face as he asked, "Mom, when can I go home and see Chris and Alison and puppy?"

His recovery from that point on was remarkable. Although Justin still battled asthma in the years to come, his treatment never required hospitalization again. When I packed his Snoopy lunch box

Lord, help me to remember that nothing is going to happen today that You and I can't handle.

—Unknown

on his first day of school, I sent him off with a deep sense of peace. I wouldn't be there to protect him.

But I knew the One who would.

And there wasn't only healing that took place in our son that day, but also in me because my focus changed from the afflicting problem to God. I saw Him anew as the all-powerful, almighty Lord for whom nothing is too difficult; as I experienced His love in the midst of the crisis, the tight grip of worry about my kids was broken. Just as God reached down inside Justin's body to restore his breathing and oxygen level, He reached deep inside of me to restore trust. Never again did I respond in panic when he had another asthma attack. As the years passed, our son still had asthma but grew stronger each year. He was a varsity tennis player for his high school and in his forties became a long-distance runner for whom marathons are a breeze—even completing rugged fifty- and seventy-mile trail runs. God has surprises around the bend as we trust Him!

LOSING CONTROL

Oh, how we wish we could control things so everything would go smoothly for us and our kids, so they wouldn't have problems and neither would we if we could just manage it all! For years, my friend Dana had prided herself on being organized, self-sufficient, and "in control" of most aspects of her life. Although she knew God, she didn't trust Him but in her ability to keep everything together. And then, she began to experience a series of adversities.

Within five years, their home was threatened by the five-hundred-year Red River flood. Her daughter fell twelve feet from the balcony of their home. Dana experienced acute health problems related to a diseased gallbladder, and her husband's business was threatened by a weakening economy. During this time they also had some uninvited visitors to their home, a home she'd kept immaculately clean. Lice! Twice! It's amazing how quickly something so small can disarm a woman who believes that she is in control of her life.

Any peace that may have come from her organizational skills and self-sufficiency soon melted away as Dana realized she was in control of absolutely nothing. She came to the end of herself, however, when their three-year-old son, Soren, began experiencing unusual spells of abdominal pain followed by lethargy and unconsciousness.

At the same time she was grieving the loss of her only son's health, she was beginning to experientially understand that the Lord cared about her, that He alone knew what her needs were, and that He would provide the exact measure of what she needed to get through each day, minute by minute. One of those provisions came in the form of a gift from a friend who gave her a first edition, original version of this book, *Trading Your Worry for Wonder*. As she read of my experience of placing my son in God's strong hands and the truth of Philippians 4:6–9, she began to see that in all things, she could:

- *pray about* what concerned her and consciously give it to God,
- *praise* Him for what He will do in the situation,
- *receive God's peace*, and
- *focus her mind* on thoughts about God.

As they received the news that their little son had a rare vascular malformation of the liver that was virtually undocumented in the history of medical literature, Dana was driven to her knees in agony and despair. At this point she realized she had to make a decision. Was she willing to place her trust in the Lord? Would she confidently entrust Soren to the Lord?

As she *prayed* about her concerns for Soren, *praised* the Lord for His power at work in his life, *received God's peace*, and *focused her mind* on the greatness and sovereignty of God, she was filled with an overwhelming sense of peace, confidence, and hope. That enabled her to confidently release her son into the Lord's hands. Little did she know this would be the beginning of a journey that is now more than five years in the making. Has God delivered them out of the adversity? No. In fact, just a few weeks ago Dana received a call at 9:30 in the morning from Soren's school saying he'd become listless during his gym class.

Dana dropped what she was doing and drove twenty minutes to the school. When she arrived, Soren was stable. As he was leaving the school office to return to class, he had another spell of lethargy. By this time, it was 11:00 a.m., and Dana was about to take her husband to the airport as he was leaving the country for a conference.

It seemed best for Soren to spend the afternoon at home. As Dana was driving, her mind was flooded with questions. *Should I take him to the emergency room? How serious is it? Should Thor leave for this conference today?* Then she remembered she was scheduled to leave town in less than forty-eight hours to assist in a weekend ministry event in Tampa, Florida. How could she possibly get on a plane and leave Soren in the hands of friends while both her husband and she would be out of town?

As she confided her fears about leaving to her prayer partner, her friend told her, "You really need to hear from the Lord on this! I will pray specifically that you will hear from Him as to whether or not you should go to Tampa." As Dana came to the Lord in prayer and continued reading the Word, she was assured God would show her what to do.

The next morning as she meditated on Psalm 102 from her daily readings, the last verse of the chapter touched her deeply: "The children of your people will live in security. Their children's children will thrive in your presence" (NLT). Although this verse brought comfort, she was still not sure that she had definitively heard from God as to whether or not she should go to Tampa.

Later that morning in Bible study, the teacher spoke from the fourth chapter of John. Dana had completed the study earlier in the week prior to Soren's spells so she wasn't prepared for the amazing new way the Lord spoke to her during the lecture. As the leader read John 4:50, Dana was awestruck. In this verse Jesus is speaking, and He says, "Go. . .your son will live" (NIV).

It was immediately apparent to Dana, and to her prayer partner sitting beside her, that the Lord had clearly spoken and she was to go to Tampa. And go, she did. Soren had a wonderful weekend with their friends and not one health problem while she was gone.

Five years into this journey with her son's health problems, Dana is still learning to trust in the Lord with all her heart. Time and time again she is learning that it is *only* as she practices praising, focusing on the Lord through prayer and the study of His Word, and receiving His peace that she has the strength for each day and hope for the future.

WORRY TO WONDER

As mothers, we have a desire to protect and care for our children that seems to come with the job description. But sometimes that caring can turn to clinging. A crisis occurs. Your child is hospitalized. The television news flashes a picture of a child kidnapped in your state or shot in a school. You become preoccupied with what might happen. You check every hour during the night to see if your baby is still breathing; you don't trust anyone to babysit. Or as a mom of teenagers, you're constantly worried about the possibility of your daughter or son getting in with the wild crowd. When these kinds of issues plague you, here are some ways to move from worry to wonder:

Release your children into God's loving hands. Praying the prayer of relinquishment as Dana and I did, essentially entrusting your kids to God, is not easy. In fact, I think letting go of our children is perhaps the hardest work of motherhood, and it may happen in a watershed moment or step by step. It may happen when your children drive off for college with all their gear, iPad, flip-flops, and many pairs of jeans piled in their car. However it occurs, releasing them to God does open a door for the Lord's power and presence to come into our children's life and the situation, and in the process we begin to be freed from chronic worry about them.

And whether you never have to go through a medical crisis with your child or not, there is a time for all of us when God asks us to do what Hannah and Abraham did: give Him what we love the most.

As Karen Mains says, "It's important for parents to walk to this spiritual altar, to offer their children back to the Lord. For many of us, this begins when they are infants. We give them to God in a dedicatory service or through a christening ceremony. We give them up to the Lord, sometimes on that first day of school watching them walk away from home, looking so small, so vulnerable before the enormous destructive forces that range the world. We suddenly realize we are not all-powerful but are dependent upon supernatural intervention to protect our children from oncoming cars, from cruelty on the playground, from harsh teachers. At each point of our children's growth, they leave us by degrees, and we must learn to give them again into God's hands."[1]

One way to move toward the goal of releasing your fears *and* your kids to God is to reflect on how faithful He has been in the past. Make a list of all His past goodness. Deena, a mother of three, hadn't ever been fearful until she had children. That changed when her infant Caitlin's lungs burst due to pulmonary hypertension and she had to be airlifted to a Houston hospital in critical condition. At that point, Deena realized how little control she had and was led to entrust her baby's medical problems to God's care. But when she got Caitlin home after many weeks in the hospital, this young mother found herself protective and clingy.

When fear and worry started to grip her again, Deena made a habit of sitting down and jotting on paper all God's past goodness in their lives. "Doing this reminds me *who my children are, who God is,* and *what He's done,*" she says.

"I remind myself they're God's children, and I'm more a caretaker for them than an owner—there's a big difference! He's *their* heavenly Father, the One who created them and promises He'll work everything in their lives for a pattern of good. And then I think of the many answered prayers, how Caitlin recovered, of the blessings that came out of difficult times. . . ."

As Deena continues listing God's goodness in this way, it's as if He loosens her grip, finger by finger, on the situation *and* the anxiety so she can trust Him in the present. As she says, "Sometimes I have as tight a grip on fear as it does on me!" Then she's free to open her hands and heart, lay her children and their problems before God, and experience His comforting presence.

Meditate on scripture to help keep your focus on the truth instead of the things that are worrying you. Pick one verse each week to add to your "Peace Packet" that specifically applies to your children or your concerns about them. (See verses at the end of this chapter to help you get started.) God's promises remind you how much He cares for you and your children. They help you remember that the One who created our children loves them more than we ever could and that they are secure in His loving, strong hands. The Bible gives us promise after promise and countless prayers that help us pray in agreement with His will and purpose for your kids.

Accept God's plan when it's different from yours. Pam

had been able to care for her daughter Jan since she was diagnosed with severe cerebral palsy as a baby. But when she was sixteen, doctors recommended she be placed in the Children's Center, a special needs long-term care facility in their city. She'd prayed to be able to take care of Jan as long as she lived. She *never* wanted to put her in a residential home. But because of her daughter's critical medical needs and her growing size, Pam could no longer care for her at home. God knew this mom's heart and her limits, and she increasingly began to realize that's why He made provision for her to be cared for in a better way than she could give. For Pam, accepting that provision brought a leap in faith and peace.

She'd worried about her daughter's suffering, afraid of not being there for her if something happened, and more. In fact, the only way Pam wasn't overwhelmed by these possibilities was to keep her eyes on God's promises and, as she puts it: "When I can't trace God's hand, I can trust His heart."

On those days when Pam saw her daughter suffering and didn't understand, she mirrored God's word back to Him, such as: "Jan's times are in Your hands. . . let me trust those times to You, Father" (Psalm 31:15).

or "Thank You, Father, that You have given Your angels charge over Jan to guard her in all her ways" (Psalm 91:11). As she prayed the promises, God increased her joy as she learned to trust Him one day at a time.

Besides visiting Jan daily at the center, Pam found tremendous ways to help the other parents of handicapped children there and began to work part-time for their church. God further widened her ministry by opening up opportunities to speak to women's groups and write a beautiful book about Jan's life. Through seeing Pam's life unfold, I've been reminded that when we let go of our expectations and are open to what God has planned, He doesn't do less but *more*, Ephesians 3:20 says. More than you could ever ask, think, or imagine, according to His riches in glory in Christ Jesus.

Faith is. . .
Confidence in God when money is running out, not rolling in.

—Pamela Reeve

Provide a prayer cover for your children. Praying for your children helps you put them in God's hands, not only in a crisis, but in everyday situations as well. Besides your own prayers for them, join with a prayer partner. Two close, faithful prayer partners have been a great source of strength to Dana; one lives 250 miles away, but once a week at 6:15 in the morning they meet by phone for a powerful time of praying together. If possible, link up with another mother who has walked with God as she faced adversity with her children. These mothers really know how to pray for you and your kids!

Prayer networks are also important when there are ongoing needs or crises—whether it's a prodigal son in harm's way or a child with medical needs like Soren. Their local church, Dana's Bible study group, and her Moms in Prayer group has been part of that network to support Soren in prayer. They also developed an electronic prayer network where they share prayer requests and praises with hundreds of friends and family here and around the world through e-mail. This enabled them to send on-the-spot requests from the Mayo Clinic and receive wonderful notes of encouragement while walking through some of the most challenging of times. Fear is banished and peace fills this mother's heart when she knows others are lifting her son to the throne of grace for God's mercy and help.

Is it your prodigal teenager that keeps your heart anxious? Never give up on a child in sin. Instead of giving up hope, ask God to give him a hunger for righteousness, take the blinders off so he will see the deception of Satan, and flood him with friends who will influence him positively for Christ. As Jean Fleming says, "Even when it seems God doesn't hear our prayers for our children, we must keep on praying persistently. Prayer may be our most effective ministry in our children's lives."[2]

WORRY BUSTERS

"All your children shall be taught by the Lord, and great shall be the peace of your children."
(ISAIAH 54:13 NKJV)

—∞—

Lord, I thank You for Your promise that You will teach my children and guide them in Your ways, and great shall be their—and my—peace.

—∞—

"For this [child] I prayed, and the Lord has given me my petition which I asked of Him. So I have also dedicated him to the Lord; as long as he lives he is dedicated to the Lord." (1 SAMUEL 1:27–28 NASB)

—∞—

Lord, just as Hannah dedicated her son Samuel to You, I dedicate and entrust my child into Your faithful, loving hands. As long as he lives, Father, he belongs to You and is dedicated to You.

—∞—

Lord, when doubts fill my mind, when my heart is in turmoil, quiet me and give me renewed hope and cheer. (PSALM 94:19 TLB)

7.

Overcoming Financial Worries

Worry is like a rocking chair.
It gives you something to do,
but it won't get you anywhere.
UNKNOWN

As we rode up the Maine highway, I felt like a fifty-pound weight was on my shoulders. My friend Linda sang along with a Christmas tape as she drove the car, but I was preoccupied with my own worried thoughts. Just then a car passed, loaded with laughing kids and brightly wrapped packages crammed into the back windshield.

It's getting so close to Christmas, I thought, *but there's no sign of Christmas money at our house this year. I don't know how I'm going to pay our rent, let alone buy the children any gifts. If we could just skip the holidays...*

The car veered toward the craggy, sharp rocks that jutted out on the right side of the highway. I braced my hands on the dashboard, and my whole body tensed up.

"Relax," Linda said. "I've driven this road a hundred times. Are you always this nervous in the car?"

"No, not until our car wreck last summer," I answered, staring out the window.

It all came rushing back as the scene flashed on the movie screen of my mind—*the curve, the motorcycle racing around the bend, heading directly toward my car... Then swerving to try to miss it. In slow-motion horror, the out-of-control motorcycle flew head-on into us, burst into flames, and slid under the van. I was thrown into the dashboard, seat belt broken. Stunned from the impact of the crash, I staggered out of the car and watched helplessly as it burned—knowing insurance wouldn't be enough to replace it.*

That car wreck had become a symbol of every out-of-control thing in my life since our move—my husband's job being downsized, the piled-up medical bills, our savings account that had withered to nothing. Lately I seemed to be worrying constantly about whether we could pay the rent or our electric bill.

The situation I faced was anxiety producing, exaggerated by the holiday season. But financial worries affect everyone in every walk of life: The farm couple who are afraid they'll lose the land that has been in the family for three generations. The small-business owner unable to make payroll. The single mom who's been told her house will be repossessed if she can't make the payment. The college student whose financial aid loans haven't come through and she doesn't know how she can make it through the semester.

If you've experienced financial worries, you're not alone. A woman alone raising children has particular stresses related to money. Many women fear that they cannot make it financially on their own if their spouse's business fails. They have a hard time believing that God really cares for them.

What can we do when finances look like they're falling apart, when we've worked hard, paid bills, and tried to save, but the rug gets pulled out from under us? That day on the highway, when I shared with my friend what was really behind my anxiety was a first step. She helped me bring my concerns to God instead of feeling ashamed for having them or discouraged about them. By getting my fears out of my head into the light of day, things didn't seem so overwhelming. What I realized then is that worry is much like an avalanche. Once the rocks or anxious thoughts start rolling, they are hard to stop, especially if we're alone with them.

> It seems to be God's plan to allow all sorts of things to happen that would naturally cause fear, but to forestall them by the assurance of His presence.
>
> —Amy Carmichael

"Friendship divides burdens and multiplies hope," someone once said. I experienced that kind of hope and encouragement as Linda and I talked and prayed together. And as I continued to turn each fearful thought into a prayer, my own perspective began to be transformed. Prayer reminds us that we're never alone, that

God is always there, ready to help us. While worry keeps us turned inward, wrapped in our own thoughts and burdens, when we turn them over to God, hope floats our heavy hearts.

Although things didn't turn around overnight in our financial situation, a few days later I felt nudged me to call the International Student Office of a local university to ask if a student who would be alone for the holidays might like to join our family. We didn't have much, but by sharing Christmas with a girl from Shanghai who was alone and ten thousand miles away from her home, a young woman who had never sung a carol or heard the Christmas story, it became one of the most meaningful, richest holidays we had experienced.

> I'd rather be in the
> palm of Your hand
> Though rich or poor I may be
> Faith can see right through
> the circumstance
> See the forest in spite
> of the trees,
> Your grace will see
> me through.
>
> —Alison Krauss

Between the invitation to Zhu Hong and Christmas weekend, a couple back home placed an order for some of my books they wanted to give as gifts, and the money I made provided enough for a gift for each person, including our international guest. . .and a turkey dinner. And I also found part-time work as a substitute teacher in the local schools, which alleviated some of the strain.

GOD IS ENOUGH

Single moms have even greater financial pressures and often no one to share them with. When Susan's husband left her and her two young girls, she had no extended family around to help or offer assistance in any way. While some single mothers have parents, aunts, or sisters to give them support, she had no one in the city they lived in.

Susan was a new believer, having accepted Christ shortly after the divorce. One night about a year after the split, she became overwhelmed by grief and guilty feelings about their failed marriage. Added to that load, intense pressures—financial and personal—had piled up and burdened her to the breaking point. It was like the weight of the world was on her shoulders.

Numb from the emotional stress of twelve-hour workdays and trying to handle all the demands of single parenting with little left to give her girls at night, she didn't know if she had the strength to go on. She called a local hospital in desperation. "I feel like I'm having a nervous breakdown. I'm anxious. I can't sleep.

Can I come in during the middle of the night if I can't make it through alone?" she asked. Just knowing she had somewhere to go for help settled her down a little.

Instead of going to the hospital, Susan glanced at her Bible on the table next to her and opened it to Isaiah 61. There she read that the Lord was sent to heal the brokenhearted. He could turn her mourning into joy and give her gratitude instead of her heavy, burdened spirit. As she read those words, it was like healing salve over her heart. She realized the strength she needed was available for her in Christ. She remembered that God had been with her all along, even when she wasn't consciously aware of His presence. And she knew He was right there with her in her lowest moments— He was her husband when there was no one else. That gave Susan the confidence to trust that God would be with her in all the challenges she faced.

Her motto became: "When you come to the point where He's all you have, you realize He's all you need." She found God was enough. His Word gave her the energy to persevere, and His Spirit guided her in every decision.

Through that guidance, she left a position in commercial real estate, which took her away from her daughters until after dark every night. She started a housecleaning business that actually provided more income and the flexibility to be home when her girls were off from school. The five-bedroom house they lived in had to be sold, but it was badly in need of repair.

Houses in their area were sitting for one to two years and selling for $10,000 lower than the asking price, so it needed to be in top condition. Instead of giving in to the what-ifs...what if I can't sell it, what if I can't afford to get it fixed up...she and her five-foot-tall cleaning assistant took off two layers of shingles and put on a new roof, laid a new linoleum floor in the kitchen, and painted the whole house inside and out. With those improvements, the house sold for only a little less than the asking price, which enabled her to buy a nice house they could afford. Every step of the process, God was right with her in a protective, strengthening way.

If Susan had depleted her energy with worry and emotional distress, there is no way she could have accomplished what she did. Maybe you've heard of the "three Ds" needed for success—desire, discipline, and determination. For Susan, it was a fourth D that provided the extra adrenaline to press on—*desperation!*

GOD, OUR PROVIDER

How could Denise, a mother of five children, cope when their family business abruptly halted? The fifteen-year-old business provided stage technicians, lighting, and labor for concerts in the city's main entertainment arena. Winters had always been a time of struggle for them because it was the slow season for concerts. But at 5:30 on a December Friday evening, they found out their entire contract for the year was canceled. Grocery money to feed their family of seven dwindled rapidly. Rent was due in a few days, and there was not enough money in their checking account to cover it. What kept her from dissolving in fear and despair?

"I've learned that the God who led the Israelites through the Red Sea is the same God who will provide and open up work for us," Denise told me. "He hasn't changed just because we've lost our job." She survived and thrived by exchanging *worry for wonder.* Like walking through a museum, we're walking through life. We don't know what life is going to bring us just like we don't know what's around the corner in a museum. Instead of worrying, she learned to be expectant and wonder: *What's God going to do next?*

Regardless of the balance in their checking account, she can get up each morning with a sense of anticipation and gratefulness because she knows God has a plan and He's cared for them in past lean times. Like the day a bread truck stopped in front of their house, and the bread man asked, "Could you use some bread? I've got a lot left over today and I've finished my route. Take whatever you want." Or the friend who called and needed home-school books, and Denise was able to sell used ones to her that day. The time neighbors down the road who prayed for their family then called saying they had an extra $250 in their savings account they wanted to give them.

Learning to "wonder" instead of worry has not been without challenge. Shortly after losing their yearly contract, they had to move out of their house because they couldn't afford the rent. However, they were able to find a large trailer home that actually met their family needs better. Denise found part-time work cleaning houses with a friend, and her husband found a temporary job.

The joy and excitement in their hearts is something only God can give as they live with a sense that

He is their Provider. A house, car, or job couldn't give that kind of joy and they won't remain. But God is going to be there no matter what.

WORRY TO WONDER

Maybe you experienced a little worry when you signed the contract for your first home and within minutes began to fear that you wouldn't have enough to make the monthly payments. Perhaps you never gave finances a thought until your husband was laid off along with a thousand other people in his high-tech company. Or your worries snowballed when creditors started calling or when you realized your kids were only a few years away from college and your savings had been eaten up. Regardless of what the situation is that triggers your rapid heartbeat, here are practical ways to move toward trust when anxiety about finances grips your heart.

> Few things make us more aware of our need for the Lord than rejection. The only final cure for the frowning face of rejection is His smiling face of love and acceptance. And the more we wait for Him, the less we'll wait in fear of future rejection.
>
> —Dr. Lloyd Ogilvie

Review who God is and write down His goodness

to you. Write in your journal all the ways God has provided in the past. Include little and big blessings. Write down things you know about God and ways you have experienced His loving-kindness, small every-day joys and gifts you've received. It can change your worry for wonder just as it did for Carol when the bottom dropped out. Her world was shaken when her husband's partnership dissolved and his health deteriorated, causing income to plummet. Any sense of security she had suddenly vaporized.

She was frightened by the financial situation, worried about her husband, afraid their house would have to be sold. For a while she just survived day to day in a fog. But when she started reviewing what she'd learned about God's nature so far and read them aloud, she discovered three truths to cling to that turned her panic to peace: *God is faithful; God is good; God loves me.*

Carol also began keeping a "Glory Journal." Looking for the good things that happened each day, no matter what difficulties she faced, she listed them in a notebook: the gorgeous colors of fall leaves, progress her son made in math class, the loving care of a friend who brought her family a dinner. The Glory Journal kept her focus on the positive and helped her avoid sliding into an abyss of negativity, discouragement, and fear.

Don't put things off. Procrastination causes more anxiety. If debts pile up because income is low, don't run from creditors (which will only make the situation worse and escalate your fears). Run toward them, but get help! Worry can cause you to delay paying bills because there may not be enough in the bank to cover them. Seek financial counseling from a reliable accountant or with a reputable credit counseling service.

Go about the business God has given you to do; for most of us, that's a full plate of responsibilities. Do the next thing. When you focus on the tasks at hand and do them, you don't have as much time to worry about what's going to happen. If you're not sure what to do, ask God, "What's my part? What am I supposed to do?"

Even if things get tough, if you follow God's principles of handling money, you can experience peace and provision. When my friend Cynthia's husband Dave lost his job, they purposed to keep following biblical principles of money management they'd learned from Larry Burkett's ministry, including a commitment to not incur any more debt—even to replace their old car or put their children through college. For her, the "fight of faith" was to keep believing and follow what God said they were to do with their money (giving, avoiding borrowing, for example) instead of jumping ship and doing things their way.

What helped Cynthia the most when she began to worry about how they would pay the bills during those lean times was to run the worst scenario and think through "What is the worst that can happen?" Then she asked herself, "Is God able?"

She decided that even if they lose their house and eat bread and water for a while, the peace God gives when they believe His promises

Maybe you have been looking for a long time for that promised "peace of God which passes all understanding" (Phil. 4:7). Today, it can radiantly transform you as you allow the stubble of mistrust to be consumed in the fire of His great love for you, through which no eternal harm can ever come.

—Barbara Sullivan

and manage money His way is worth more than things, than a big car or vacation. That peace comes not by having everything they want, but by living simply and following biblical principles of finance. She realized and believed that while we can never command God to do what we want, if we're managing money His way, then when crisis comes, we have a strong foundation, and things don't get chaotic.

In facing her fears this way, she finds herself energized to wait on God, to do her part, and to see how He guides. And you know what? Their family of six never missed any meals—she's the best cook I know! They not only had enough to feed their own children, but to offer hospitality and warm meals to countless people over the years they've invited into their home.

Personalize the promises of scripture and fear will flee. When you're tempted to speak anxiously about your financial situation, exchange your thoughts for the truth. For example, instead of saying, "We'll never have enough; things are just getting worse," affirm: "We have everything we need to live a life that pleases God. It was all given to us by God's own power when we learned that He had invited us to share in His wonderful goodness!" (see 2 Peter 1:3). Adding verses like these to your Peace Packet that specifically apply to money matters and God's provision can help you face challenging financial times:

> *"So do not worry, saying, 'What shall we eat?' or 'What shall we drink?' or 'What shall we wear?'*

For the pagans run after all these things, and your heavenly Father knows that you need them. But seek first his kingdom and his righteousness, and all these things will be given to you as well. Therefore do not worry about tomorrow."
(MATTHEW 6:31–34 NIV)

I was young and now I am old, yet I have never seen the righteous forsaken or their children begging bread. (PSALM 37:25 NIV)

"Give, and it will be given to you. A good measure, pressed down, shaken together and running over, will be poured into your lap. For with the measure you use, it will be measured to you."
(LUKE 6:38 NIV)

The young lions do lack and suffer hunger; but they who seek the LORD shall not be in want of any good thing. (PSALM 34:10 NASB)

As you meditate on God's promises daily, say the verse in your own words, telling God you are depending on Him. Then continue to add promises from your own

Bible reading that build your confidence in God and His ability to provide.

Share the burdens. Even the wealthy aren't always exempt from financial worries. I heard a financial consultant once say that prosperity leads to fear of loss, and fear of loss leads to loss of faith. Whatever your anxieties or concerns are about finances, give them to God one by one and be specific about your needs. Talk and pray about these heavy burdens with a friend. If worried thoughts about your financial situation resurface, which they often do, give them back to God right then. Release them as many times as necessary until your mind is free from fretting about them.

Let me encourage you to avoid being like the little boy who took his broken bicycle to the repair shop to be fixed. The repairman assured him it would be as good as new, and told him to leave his bike in the repair room. He promised to call when he was finished fixing it. But after being home for a day or two, the boy began to worry about his bike: *Can the repairman really fix the problem? Is he going to call me or lose my bike? Why isn't it ready yet?* Before he knew it, the little boy raced down to the shop and reclaimed his bicycle— still broken.

You and I are much like that boy. We may give our financial problem to God, but moments or hours later, we take it back and start handling it ourselves. If you find you've reclaimed your "broken bike," or broken money matters, give them back to God. . .and leave them there!

WORRY BUSTERS

The LORD is my shepherd, I lack nothing.
(PSALM 23:1 NIV)

—∞—

God, you are my Shepherd. You give me everything I need so I won't be in want.

—∞—

Remember this: Whoever sows sparingly will also reap sparingly, and whoever sows generously will also reap generously. Each of you should give what you have decided in your heart to give, not

*reluctantly or under compulsion, for God loves
a cheerful giver. And God is able to bless you
abundantly, so that in all things at all times,
having all that you need, you will abound in
every good work.* (2 CORINTHIANS 9:6–8 NIV)

—⁂—

Lord, You are able to make all grace abound to me, so
that in all things at all times, having all that I need, I will
abound in every good work. Help me to be a cheerful
giver and follow Your ways of handling whatever
money or resources are entrusted to me. Empower me
to sow generously and reap generously and to always
give You the praise from a thankful heart for all You
have provided and blessed me with.

—⁂—

Now to him who is able to do immeasurably more than all we ask or imagine, according to his power that is at work within us, to him be glory in the church and in Christ Jesus throughout all generations, for ever and ever!
(EPHESIANS 3:20–21 NIV)

—⁊⁊—

Father, help me remember that You are able to do immeasurably more than all I could ask or imagine, according to Your mighty power at work within me. To You be glory forever and ever!

8.

Overcoming Worries about Relationships

There is no fear in love. But perfect love drives out fear, because fear has to do with punishment. The one who fears is not made perfect in love. We love because he first loved us.

1 JOHN 4:18–19 NIV

When you can't trust God, it's very hard to trust any-one else, especially your husband. And that lack of trust can damage relationships. I found this out by personal experience. In fact, my anxiety threatened to ruin our first Christmas together. Holmes and I were on our way back from Wellington, Kansas, to Dallas for a New Year's Eve celebration of my mother's birthday. It was December 1969, and we had only been married one month. Little did Holmes know the basket case of nerves he would have sitting beside him in the car.

Since almost everyone in my family had a touch of "car anxiety," I thought it normal the way my big sister threw her arms on the dashboard when she thought I was stopping too close to the car in front or how we were all such experts at backseat driving. After all, we four sisters had been on the fateful trip to Ruidoso, New Mexico, when my sister Georgia fell asleep leaning on the car door and went flying out on the highway. Mama, with me in her arms, became hysterical and ran back to get her. Papa, normally reserved, was shaken as he scooped my bloody, unconscious sister up in his arms. He declared that we'd never take another family trip—and we didn't, as long as he lived. Georgia survived with only abrasions from head to foot, but car anxiety was the long-term effect for all the rest of us in the car.

Holmes and I drove away from his grandparents' house, waving and smiling, excited about getting back to Dallas and our little duplex in Waco as the first snowflakes were beginning to fall. It was our first New Year's Eve as a couple. Having grown up in Dallas where we saw snow only once in five years, I loved the way the Kansas countryside looked as we drove by the wheat fields now growing whiter and whiter. But my delight turned to worry as the snow blanketed the road and the highway grew slicker. Holmes felt confident about driving us back to Texas safely; he'd had lots of experience driving on snow and ice while growing up in northern Oklahoma. Besides, to him this was a great adventure, and he loved adventures.

However, I was petrified as daylight turned to darkness and our car began sliding on the icy roads.

> Maybe you have been looking for a long time for that promised "peace of God which passes all understanding" (Phil. 4:7). Today, it can radiantly transform you as you allow the stubble of mistrust to be consumed in the fire of His great love for you, through which no eternal harm can ever come.
>
> —Barbara Sullivan

Miss White-Knuckle-Door-Handle-Hugger clung to it as if somehow gripping it could save me

"Holmes, please slow down!" I said, anxiety rising up and choking me.

"I'm only going twenty-five miles per hour," he answered. "Relax."

Relax! I thought. This looked like a full-scale blizzard to me, and we could barely see anything ahead for the whirlwind of white covering the windshield. There was *no way* I could relax. My foot "braked" to slow us down, but that didn't work. It felt like we were going too fast. But even five miles per hour would have been too fast for me. I was so scared I could barely speak except to say an occasional, "Slow down!"

Holmes ignored me and kept driving steadily along. As we cruised through several small towns, snow drifted in huge piles. Only one lane was open. Cars were careening off the road because under the snow was a solid sheet of ice. But whenever we slid off the road, Holmes somehow got us back on track and kept going.

"Holmes, why don't we just stop?"

"We don't have the option of stopping. We're between towns, and it's too cold to pull to the side of the road. Besides, we'd freeze."

"Then let's spend the night in the next little town and continue driving in the morning when the roads are better." As soon as we went through the next one, we passed several motels, but they all had No Vacancy signs out. My spirits fell.

"Look! There's a sign saying travelers can stay at the high school gymnasium overnight because of the snowstorm," I said, thinking that was a great idea.

"Your family is expecting us for your mom and sister's birthday party, and I'm not about to sleep on a cold, hard gym floor tonight."

As much as I loved a family party, sleeping on a gym floor sounded better to me than six more hours of this stressful driving. And plenty of cars were turning into the school ahead of us who agreed.

"There's no reason to stop," he bristled. "We're fine, and I can get us to Dallas safely."

With each mile Holmes grew more irritated by my nervousness. I felt hurt because he didn't understand my fear. He didn't appreciate my "backseat driving." He didn't feel affirmed since I wasn't admiring his driving skills. I was upset he wouldn't drive slower. And he thought he *was* driving carefully and felt criticized.

Anger, fear, and hurt welled up in me and neither of us could relate to the other!

When we finally arrived at my parents' home in Dallas well after midnight that New Year's Eve, I was worn out from the stressful drive (even though I hadn't done any of the driving. Worry will do that to you—drain all your energy), and Holmes and I were barely speaking. Unfortunately, this was a scene that occurred several times in the early years of our marriage. Between the normally peace-loving, low-conflict two of us, some of our worst times were in the car.

> It is the law of the spiritual life that every act of trust makes the next act less difficult, until at length, if these acts are persisted in, trusting becomes, like breathing, the natural unconscious action of the redeemed soul.
>
> —Hannah Whitall Smith

GOD INTERVENES

I don't know where we'd have ended up if God hadn't intervened in our marriage, because my fears plus all our other emotional baggage were putting a big strain on the relationship. But one of the wonderful things about God is that He knows all about us and loves us anyway. He knows our needs even before we ask and knows what is underneath our weaknesses when we are clueless. And when we let Him, God can marvelously transform our fears and heal our hurts.

As Holmes and I grew spiritually, we gradually gave God more and more of our lives: habits, finances, careers. We told the Lord we'd go any direction He wanted, and He opened up new doors for Holmes. He was so faithful, we eventually gave Him our marriage. We knew we needed help and healing. After all, in eight years of trying to do life on our own, a lot of resentment and negative patterns had built up. But since we couldn't afford counseling, we had no idea how anything could change.

In 1978, Holmes and I attended a weekend conference that focused on restoration of the family, church, and nation. We were inspired by hearing Peter Marshall speak, and on Sunday a healing service was planned. Although we'd never heard of a healing service, it sounded like a good idea. Despite all efforts with medication, allergy shots, and diet changes, our son's asthma was still a struggle, so this invitation to have someone pray for him sounded great.

On Sunday afternoon we sat with our children at the back of the auditorium with several hundred other people to hear the message. Then we were instructed to write our prayer request on paper provided in the bulletin and come up to one of the three ministers to be prayed for.

After a wise, older pastor shared about what the Bible had to say about healing, I thought he looked like the best person. So I wrote, "Our son has severe asthma and chronic allergies that has caused trips to the ER and hospital since he was four. Could you pray for him?" and we hesitantly got in the pastor's line. However, his line was so long that we were steered over to Peter Marshall.

We sat down on the pew before him when it was our turn for prayer. Reverend Marshall didn't know us, but he looked intently down the row at each of us and at our son. Then he looked back at me and said, "*You're* the one who really needs prayer. Come up and let me pray for you."

But you don't understand, I thought. *It's not me—it's our son who needs prayer for his asthma. That's what we came for.* Not one to argue with the person in charge, we walked up and he began.

"Lord, heal the heart of this young woman who lost her father as a child. Take away her sense of being abandoned by her father and You...," he began to pray. Why, I hadn't told him anything about my dad's dying when I was young.

Somehow God gave this man who had lost his own father when he was ten years old the knowledge that losing my father when I was a child left me with a sense of being abandoned, resulting in a lack of trust in my husband and in God. He asked the Lord to heal all those emotions and to see how faithful my heavenly Father is, how He'd led me and protected me all through my life. He asked for trust to be rebuilt between me and my husband. As he prayed, it was like the deep root system of worry, fear, and distrust was literally lifted out of my soul.

And as he continued praying, my reserved husband began to weep uncontrollably, the hurt literally pouring out of him for my never trusting him to drive safely enough or handle decisions. I'd never seen Holmes cry like this in our whole marriage. Resentment and irritations were washed from both of us as the tears flowed. Peter continued praying for our marriage to be healed and for us to truly "cleave" to one another and become one.

At the close of the weekend, when we stood with

other couples to renew our vows, we felt like the old passed away and we had a brand-new start to our relationship.

And although our son was not prayed for as *my* plan was, his asthma did begin to improve. I got a new glimpse of my heavenly Father that day and was filled with awe and wonder that He was so caring that he sent a man like Peter Marshall from way across the country, a man I'd never met whose father had died when he was a child, just as mine had, to minister to the deepest part of my heart and bring freedom.

Fear Hinders Relationships

Because of the over 50 percent divorce rate, many women were raised without fathers. Some feel they can't depend on a man or commit to a relationship. But "today's widespread fear of trusting men can actually become the catalyst that causes us to place our trust and faith in God. The stress that comes when we attempt to be in control of relationships will ultimately rob us of the joy of life. We can become free of that stress when we release our control to God and begin to live in freedom from fear," says Barbara Sullivan in *The Control Trap*.[1]

Maybe your fear isn't a lack of trust in a person as I experienced, but a fear of being abandoned or rejected. That kind of fear usually causes a woman to build walls around her heart, and in the process she grows lonelier and lonelier. Or fear of rejection may lead her to people pleasing and being taken advantage of by friends and family. "One of my biggest worries is investing time and heart in a friendship and then seeing my friend marry and move away," said one single woman. "It's happened over and over, and I come up empty." Some fear being used, being betrayed, being alone, or not measuring up to what others think they should be.

One of the main places a fear of rejection comes from is from our early experiences with family. As Stephen Arterburn, Paul Meier, and Robert L. Wise say, "Parents are of supreme importance to all of us as children. We desperately need our parents' love and want to know we mean the world to Mom *and* Dad. When unconditional love isn't possible, the door opens to a deeply unsettling fear our parents may be about to jettison us out of their lives. Such fear of rejection is terrifying!"[2]

Ever since she was a little girl, Stephanie had struggled with this kind of rejection. Her father would say over and over to her and her sister, "Nobody loves you like your daddy," but he was the one who forgot to pick her up from school in the first grade. . .ignored her birthdays. . .wasn't at the airport when she flew home to visit him in high school. Her dad also had girlfriends about four years older than Stephanie to take her to the mall when it was his court-ordered visitation day.

Not having a relationship with her dad left a hole in Stephanie's heart, and she carried a yearning for a father figure into adulthood. It also caused her to unconsciously pick a "substitute for the rejecting parent,"[3] first a handsome guy who turned out to be a drug addict, and two years later, a knight in shining armor who swept her off her feet but once they were married mentally, physically, and sexually abused her. After fourteen months, that marriage was over. Still she kept praying daily that God would send her someone to love.

Folding laundry one Saturday afternoon, she lamented her marital situation. Her emotions over the past year had run the gamut from rage, abandonment, fear, and sorrow, to hopelessness. She began to blame her suffering on God. Crying uncontrollably, she fell to her knees. *Why did You do this to me? Why? Why, God?*

"You prayed for Someone you could love," was the reply of the Almighty as she heard Him whisper to her heart. All of a sudden, the tears stopped. She'd thought romantic love was the answer. . .the solution to the emptiness in her life. It was as though God said, *"You asked Me to show you how to love. . .I am giving you more than this man. . .I am teaching you to love Me."* She realized then that unfortunately there had been no room in her heart for God until her heart was broken by a mortal man. Slowly she began to learn to love God who always returns her love and never breaks her heart. As the old fears of rejection and abandonment and loss were healed, a place was eventually made for a healthy relationship with a godly, loving man, her darling husband Michael.

Instead of looking for love in all the wrong places as Stephanie did, other people cope with fear of rejection by withdrawing and retreating from any attempt to love or be loved. "We seek safety in going unnoticed. We reach out to no one lest we be rebuffed. Jesus commanded the disciples to 'love one another as I have loved you' (John 15:12 RSV). Shyness utterly stifles the ability to do that and, in that sense, could be considered a sin," says Bruce Larson in *Living Beyond Our Fears.*[4]

WORRY TO WONDER

Instead of withdrawing, substituting, retreating, or letting our fears harm our relationships, we can let these struggles drive us to the cross. For as Larson says, "Fear is the handle by which we lay hold of God."[5] Laying hold of God enables us to receive His love for us—an unfailing, unconditional, powerful love that drives out the dread of rejection and enables us to be vessels of love to others.

Experience God's love. As the little verse goes, "Do you love me, or do you not? You told me once, but I forgot." Many of us have heard a lot about God's love. We've read about His love and seen His love in other people's lives. But have we experienced God's love in a way that brings our hearts to rest?

One Sunday just as we were singing the words, "There's no place I'd rather be in your arms of love, in your arms of love, holding me still, holding me near in your arms of love,"[6] I noticed Bonnie, a third grader I'd taught in children's church, going up and down the aisles, looking for her dad. Bonnie had a bewildered look on her face as she passed each row, but she was persistently looking up and down each one until she found him.

Finally she arrived at our aisle and saw her daddy a few seats down from me. She took off, climbing around me and several others. She literally leaped up in his arms and rested her head on her father's shoulder. As the song continued, he held her small hand in his and the biggest smile I've ever seen lit her face up. She was *home!* This picture of what we were singing struck me: God wants our hearts to come home to Him— He wants us to feel that same kind of daddy love as Bonnie did with her dad, only much more.

First John 4:18 tells us that we don't have to fear someone who loves us perfectly as God does. Or as the Message translation puts it, "There is no room in love for fear. Well-formed love banishes fear." Knowing His complete and total love for us delivers us from any dread or worry of what He might do to us or what life would deal us! It frees us from having to please people or being afraid they'll reject us or abandon us to truly love.

David knew what it was like to be misunderstood by friends and family and pursued by enemies who betrayed him. But despite rejection and discouragement, he proclaimed, "No one who hopes in you will ever be put to shame" (Psalm 25:3 NIV). No matter what people did or how they treated him, his hope was in the Lord.

This leads us to a much greater, more eternal reason to know God than just living a life free of fear. Knowing God through trusting our life to the lordship of Jesus Christ is an end in itself. In fact, it is *the end, the purpose for which we were created*, as the ancient tradition of the Heidelberg Catechism states: "The chief end of man is to glorify God and to enjoy Him forever."

As A. W. Tozer said, "God is not asking you to come to Christ just to attain peace of mind or to make you a better businessman or woman. You were created to worship. God wants you to know His redemption so you will desire to worship and praise Him."[7] What a great invitation. If you don't know God, take time to ask Christ to forgive your sins, to reveal Himself to you and come into your heart, and to fit you for heaven so you will live with Him forever.

Verbally share your fear with someone else. When we confess what we're afraid of, whether that is "I don't know if I'll ever get married," or "I'm afraid I won't ever have a close friend again," our anxiety shrinks to a manageable size and solutions begin to come into view. Sometimes we need professional help to discover why we're afraid of people or why we fear rejection. But little by little we can gain insight into the roots of distrust as we talk them over with a counselor or a trusted mentor.

When we hide the fear inside our head, it multiplies and isolates us from other people. When we acknowledge instead of deny or cover up our fear with some self-defeating strategy, it can propel us into pursuing God and healthy relationships.

Look to God's Word to discover who you are in Christ. At the very heart of our fear of rejection are the misbeliefs we hold about ourselves. Go to God's love letter to you, the Bible, and exchange every misbelief or lie about yourself with the truth about who you are in Christ. Overrule what you think or feel with what is true about you according to scripture. For example: if you think, *I am unworthy and unacceptable*, God's Word says that in Christ, *you are accepted and worthy* in Psalm 139:14: "I am fearfully and wonderfully made; your works are wonderful, I know that full well" (NIV). In saying this, we do not praise ourselves—*we praise God* for how He made us and the purpose He has for us.

When you feel *There is nothing special about me*, remember that God says you have been chosen and set apart by Him. Not because you are so great without

Him (actually we are nothing without Him), but because you belong to Him: "It is because of Him that you are in Christ Jesus, who has become for us wisdom from God—that is, our righteousness, holiness and redemption" (1 Corinthians 1:30 NIV). Also, see Ephesians 1:4 and Hebrews 10:10 and 10:14.

As my friend, counselor Leslie Vernick, says, "Part of building a proper picture of ourselves is to see ourselves truthfully, as much-loved sinners, not as wonderful persons." Romans 5:8 says, "God demonstrates his own love for us in this: While we were still sinners, Christ died for us" (NIV).

When you think, *I am unwanted* or *I don't belong to anyone*, review the truth that you have been adopted by God Himself and you are His child. (See Romans 8:16–17, Galatians 4:5, and 1 John 3:2.) As you focus your mind on the truth, a confident sense of "Christ-consciousness"[8] will replace your self-consciousness and you will be freer to love others, love God, and yourself.

Combat the fear of rejection or loneliness by becoming an encourager. Like Barnabas, one of my favorite New Testament heroes, we can become an encourager of others. As Hebrews states: "Let us consider how we may spur one another on toward love and good deeds, not giving up meeting together, as some are in the habit of doing, but encouraging one another—and all the more as you see the Day approaching" (Hebrews 10:24–25 NIV).

When you set your focus on giving the gift of encouragement by showing appreciation for others, writing a note of thanks, and delivering help, support, hope, kindness, reassurance, and faith to others (for that's what the word *encouragement* means), loneliness begins to flee and your heart, having given much, receives much.

WORRY BUSTERS

God is love, and all who live in love live in God, and God lives in them. And as we live in God, our love grows more perfect. So we will not be afraid on the day of judgment, but we can face him with confidence because we live like Christ here in this world. Such love has no fear, because perfect love expels all fear. . . . We love each other because he loved us first. (I JOHN 4:16–19 NLT)

—※—

Lord, thank You for loving me first so I could know You. Here are the fears I have concerning relationships: I give them all to You. I want Your love to be the anchor of my relationships and my life. Help me to live and abide in You and for Your perfect love to cast out all fear from my heart, my emotions, and my mind. Then empower me to love other people as a result of Your love living in me.

—※—

When I am afraid,
I will put my trust in You.
In God, whose word I praise,
In God I have put my trust;
I shall not be afraid. (Psalm 56:3–4 NASB)

—※—

Father God, when I am afraid, I make the choice and set my will to trust in You and Your Word. I praise

Your Word, which strengthens me and frees me from fear of what others might do to me. I praise Your faithfulness, which assures me that You are always with me. No matter what enemies surround me, I don't have to fear or be afraid. I can walk in Your presence, in Your life-giving light! Thank You, Lord!

Endnotes

Chapter 1

[1] *Oxford Dictionaries*, s.v. "worry," http://www.oxford-dictionaries.com/definition/english/worry.

[2] Nancy Travers, LCSW, "Is It Worry, Anxiety, or Panic? Why Women Worry So Much," www.4therapy.com, 1.

[3] Travers, "Is It Worry, Anxiety, or Panic?," 1.

[4] From a report by the Australian Psychological Society reported in www.man.bodyandsoul.com, 1.

[5] Travers, "Is It Worry, Anxiety, or Panic?," 1.

[6] Melanie Haiken, "Do You Worry Too Much? 7 Ways Worrying Sabotages Your Career," *Forbes.com*, September 18, 2013, http://www.forbes.com/sites/melaniehaiken/2013/09/18/are-you-worrying-your-way-out-of-a-job-7-ways-worrying-hurts-women-in-the-workplace/, 1.

[7] Paul Tournier, quoted in Keith Miller and Bruce Larson, *The Edge of Adventure* (Waco, TX: Word Books, 1976), 180.

Chapter 2

[1] Gary Thomas, "Finding Fortitude," *Discipleship Journal*, no. 130 (July/August 2002): 38.

[2] Corrie ten Boom, *Reflections of God's Glory* (Grand Rapids: Zondervan, 1999), 91–92.

[3] Ruth Myers, *31 Days of Praise* (Singapore: The Navigators, 1992), 19.

[4] Myers, *31 Days of Praise*, 19.

[5] Fern Nichols, *Heart to Heart* newsletter, vol. 7 (1995): 1.

[6] Dave Shive, "You've Got to Fear Somebody," *Discipleship Journal*, no. 130 (July/August 2002): 44.

Chapter 3

Judson Cornwall, *Praying the Scriptures: Using God's Words to Effect Change in All of Life's Situations* (Lake Mary: Charisma House, 2008), x-xi

Chapter 4

[1] Robert Jamieson, quoted in Cynthia Heald, *Abiding in Christ* (Colorado Springs: NavPress, 1995), 44.

Chapter 5

[1] Hannah Hurnard, *Hind's Feet on High Places* (Wheaton, IL: Tyndale House, 1975), 11–12.

[2] Quote adapted from "Singing Like Myself," blog post by shabbyblogs.com (1/21/08), http://singinglikemyself.blogspot.com/2008/01/praise-at-all-times.html

[3] Fenelon, *Let Go* (Springdale, PA: Whitaker House, 1973), 3.

[4] David Wilkerson, "Bringing Christ into Your Crisis," Times Square Church Pulpit Series, January 1, 1996, 4.

[5] Catherine Marshall, *Adventures in Prayer* (New York: Ballantine Books, 1975), 63.

[6] Quote taken from "Encouraging Words," blog post by Cary Schmidt (July 2010), http://caryschmidt.com/2010/03/andrew-murray-on-trials/

Chapter 6

[1] Karen Burton Mains, "Sacrificing Our Isaacs," in *One Holy Passion*, ed. Judith Couchman (Colorado Springs, CO: Waterbrook, 1998), 138.

[2] Jean Fleming, *A Mother's Heart: A Look at Values, Vision, and Character for the Christian Mother* (Colorado Springs: NavPress, 1996), x.

Chapter 8

[1] Barbara Sullivan, *The Control Trap* (Minneapolis, MN: Bethany House, 1991), 79, 81.

[2] Stephen Arterburn, Paul Meier, and Robert L. Wise, *Fear Less for Life* (Nashville: Thomas Nelson, 2002), 57.

[3] Arterburn et al., *Fear Less for Life*, 58.

[4] Bruce Larson, *Living Beyond Our Fears*, (New York: HarperColins, 1990), 128.

[5] Larson, *Living Beyond Our Fears*, 150.

[6] Song lyrics courtesy of Mercy Publishing, 1991.

[7] A. W. Tozer, *Whatever Happened to Worship?* (Camp Hill, PA: Christian Publications, 1982), 91.

[8] The term *Christ-consciousness* is adapted from Larson, *Living Beyond Our Fears*, 131.

Read Through the Bible in a Year

1-Jan	Gen. 1-2	Matt. 1	Ps. 1
2-Jan	Gen. 3-4	Matt. 2	Ps. 2
3-Jan	Gen. 5-7	Matt. 3	Ps. 3
4-Jan	Gen. 8-10	Matt. 4	Ps. 4
5-Jan	Gen. 11-13	Matt. 5:1-20	Ps. 5
6-Jan	Gen. 14-16	Matt. 5:21-48	Ps. 6
7-Jan	Gen. 17-18	Matt. 6:1-18	Ps. 7
8-Jan	Gen. 19-20	Matt. 6:19-34	Ps. 8
9-Jan	Gen. 21-23	Matt. 7:1-11	Ps. 9:1-8
10-Jan	Gen. 24	Matt. 7:12-29	Ps. 9:9-20
11-Jan	Gen. 25-26	Matt. 8:1-17	Ps. 10:1-11
12-Jan	Gen. 27:1-28:9	Matt. 8:18-34	Ps. 10:12-18
13-Jan	Gen. 28:10-29:35	Matt. 9	Ps. 11
14-Jan	Gen. 30:1-31:21	Matt. 10:1-15	Ps. 12
15-Jan	Gen. 31:22-32:21	Matt. 10:16-36	Ps. 13
16-Jan	Gen. 32:22-34:31	Matt. 10:37-11:6	Ps. 14
17-Jan	Gen. 35-36	Matt. 11:7-24	Ps. 15
18-Jan	Gen. 37-38	Matt. 11:25-30	Ps. 16
19-Jan	Gen. 39-40	Matt. 12:1-29	Ps. 17
20-Jan	Gen. 41	Matt. 12:30-50	Ps. 18:1-15
21-Jan	Gen. 42-43	Matt. 13:1-9	Ps. 18:16-29
22-Jan	Gen. 44-45	Matt. 13:10-23	Ps. 18:30-50
23-Jan	Gen. 46:1-47:26	Matt. 13:24-43	Ps. 19
24-Jan	Gen. 47:27-49:28	Matt. 13:44-58	Ps. 20
25-Jan	Gen. 49:29-Exod. 1:22	Matt. 14	Ps. 21
26-Jan	Exod. 2-3	Matt. 15:1-28	Ps. 22:1-21
27-Jan	Exod. 4:1-5:21	Matt. 15:29-16:12	Ps. 22:22-31
28-Jan	Exod. 5:22-7:24	Matt. 16:13-28	Ps. 23
29-Jan	Exod. 7:25-9:35	Matt. 17:1-9	Ps. 24
30-Jan	Exod. 10-11	Matt. 17:10-27	Ps. 25
31-Jan	Exod. 12	Matt. 18:1-20	Ps. 26
1-Feb	Exod. 13-14	Matt. 18:21-35	Ps. 27
2-Feb	Exod. 15-16	Matt. 19:1-15	Ps. 28
3-Feb	Exod. 17-19	Matt. 19:16-30	Ps. 29
4-Feb	Exod. 20-21	Matt. 20:1-19	Ps. 30
5-Feb	Exod. 22-23	Matt. 20:20-34	Ps. 31:1-8

6-Feb	Exod. 24-25	Matt. 21:1-27	Ps. 31:9-18
7-Feb	Exod 26-27	Matt. 21:28-46	Ps. 31:19-24
8-Feb	Exod. 28	Matt. 22	Ps. 32
9-Feb	Exod. 29	Matt. 23:1-36	Ps. 33:1-12
10-Feb	Exod. 30-31	Matt. 23:37-24:28	Ps. 33:13-22
11-Feb	Exod. 32-33	Matt. 24:29-51	Ps. 34:1-7
12-Feb	Exod. 34:1-35:29	Matt. 25:1-13	Ps. 34:8-22
13-Feb	Exod. 35:30-37:29	Matt. 25:14-30	Ps. 35:1-8
14-Feb	Exod. 38-39	Matt. 25:31-46	Ps. 35:9-17
15-Feb	Exod. 40	Matt. 26:1-35	Ps. 35:18-28
16-Feb	Lev. 1-3	Matt. 26:36-68	Ps. 36:1-6
17-Feb	Lev. 4:1-5:13	Matt. 26:69-27:26	Ps. 36:7-12
18-Feb	Lev. 5:14 -7:21	Matt. 27:27-50	Ps. 37:1-6
19-Feb	Lev. 7:22-8:36	Matt. 27:51-66	Ps. 37:7-26
20-Feb	Lev. 9-10	Matt. 28	Ps. 37:27-40
21-Feb	Lev. 11-12	Mark 1:1-28	Ps. 38
22-Feb	Lev. 13	Mark 1:29-39	Ps. 39
23-Feb	Lev. 14	Mark 1:40-2:12	Ps. 40:1-8
24-Feb	Lev. 15	Mark 2:13-3:35	Ps. 40:9-17
25-Feb	Lev. 16-17	Mark 4:1-20	Ps. 41:1-4
26-Feb	Lev. 18-19	Mark 4:21-41	Ps. 41:5-13
27-Feb	Lev. 20	Mark 5	Ps. 42-43
28-Feb	Lev. 21-22	Mark 6:1-13	Ps. 44
1-Mar	Lev. 23-24	Mark 6:14-29	Ps. 45:1-5
2-Mar	Lev. 25	Mark 6:30-56	Ps. 45:6-12
3-Mar	Lev. 26	Mark 7	Ps. 45:13-17
4-Mar	Lev. 27	Mark 8	Ps. 46
5-Mar	Num. 1-2	Mark 9:1-13	Ps. 47
6-Mar	Num. 3	Mark 9:14-50	Ps. 48:1-8
7-Mar	Num. 4	Mark 10:1-34	Ps. 48:9-14
8-Mar	Num. 5:1-6:21	Mark 10:35-52	Ps. 49:1-9
9-Mar	Num. 6:22-7:47	Mark 11	Ps. 49:10-20
10-Mar	Num. 7:48-8:4	Mark 12:1-27	Ps. 50:1-15
11-Mar	Num. 8:5-9:23	Mark 12:28-44	Ps. 50:16-23
12-Mar	Num. 10-11	Mark 13:1-8	Ps. 51:1-9
13-Mar	Num. 12-13	Mark 13:9-37	Ps. 51:10-19

14-Mar	Num. 14	Mark 14:1-31	Ps. 52
15-Mar	Num. 15	Mark 14:32-72	Ps. 53
16-Mar	Num. 16	Mark 15:1-32	Ps. 54
17-Mar	Num. 17-18	Mark 15:33-47	Ps. 55
18-Mar	Num. 19-20	Mark 16	Ps. 56:1-7
19-Mar	Num. 21:1-22:20	Luke 1:1-25	Ps. 56:8-13
20-Mar	Num. 22:21-23:30	Luke 1:26-56	Ps. 57
21-Mar	Num. 24-25	Luke 1:57-2:20	Ps. 58
22-Mar	Num. 26:1-27:11	Luke 2:21-38	Ps. 59:1-8
23-Mar	Num. 27:12-29:11	Luke 2:39-52	Ps. 59:9-17
24-Mar	Num. 29:12-30:16	Luke 3	Ps. 60:1-5
25-Mar	Num. 31	Luke 4	Ps. 60:6-12
26-Mar	Num. 32-33	Luke 5:1-16	Ps. 61
27-Mar	Num. 34-36	Luke 5:17-32	Ps. 62:1-6
28-Mar	Deut. 1:1-2:25	Luke 5:33-6:11	Ps. 62:7-12
29-Mar	Deut. 2:26-4:14	Luke 6:12-35	Ps. 63:1-5
30-Mar	Deut. 4:15-5:22	Luke 6:36-49	Ps. 63:6-11
31-Mar	Deut. 5:23-7:26	Luke 7:1-17	Ps. 64:1-5
1-Apr	Deut. 8-9	Luke 7:18-35	Ps. 64:6-10
2-Apr	Deut. 10-11	Luke 7:36-8:3	Ps. 65:1-8
3-Apr	Deut. 12-13	Luke 8:4-21	Ps. 65:9-13
4-Apr	Deut. 14:1-16:8	Luke 8:22-39	Ps. 66:1-7
5-Apr	Deut. 16:9-18:22	Luke 8:40-56	Ps. 66:8-15
6-Apr	Deut. 19:1-21:9	Luke 9:1-22	Ps. 66:16-20
7-Apr	Deut. 21:10-23:8	Luke 9:23-42	Ps. 67
8-Apr	Deut. 23:9-25:19	Luke 9:43-62	Ps. 68:1-6
9-Apr	Deut. 26:1-28:14	Luke 10:1-20	Ps. 68:7-14
10-Apr	Deut. 28:15-68	Luke 10:21-37	Ps. 68:15-19
11-Apr	Deut. 29-30	Luke 10:38-11:23	Ps. 68:20-27
12-Apr	Deut. 31:1-32:22	Luke 11:24-36	Ps. 68:28-35
13-Apr	Deut. 32:23-33:29	Luke 11:37-54	Ps. 69:1-9
14-Apr	Deut. 34-Josh. 2	Luke 12:1-15	Ps. 69:10-17
15-Apr	Josh. 3:1-5:12	Luke 12:16-40	Ps. 69:18-28
16-Apr	Josh. 5:13-7:26	Luke 12:41-48	Ps. 69:29-36
17-Apr	Josh. 8-9	Luke 12:49-59	Ps. 70
18-Apr	Josh. 10:1-11:15	Luke 13:1-21	Ps. 71:1-6

19-Apr	Josh. 11:16-13:33	Luke 13:22-35	Ps. 71:7-16
20-Apr	Josh. 14-16	Luke 14:1-15	Ps. 71:17-21
21-Apr	Josh. 17:1-19:16	Luke 14:16-35	Ps. 71:22-24
22-Apr	Josh. 19:17-21:42	Luke 15:1-10	Ps. 72:1-11
23-Apr	Josh. 21:43-22:34	Luke 15:11-32	Ps. 72:12-20
24-Apr	Josh. 23-24	Luke 16:1-18	Ps. 73:1-9
25-Apr	Judg. 1-2	Luke 16:19-17:10	Ps. 73:10-20
26-Apr	Judg. 3-4	Luke 17:11-37	Ps. 73:21-28
27-Apr	Judg. 5:1-6:24	Luke 18:1-17	Ps. 74:1-3
28-Apr	Judg. 6:25-7:25	Luke 18:18-43	Ps. 74:4-11
29-Apr	Judg. 8:1-9:23	Luke 19:1-28	Ps. 74:12-17
30-Apr	Judg. 9:24-10:18	Luke 19:29-48	Ps. 74:18-23
1-May	Judg. 11:1-12:7	Luke 20:1-26	Ps. 75:1-7
2-May	Judg. 12:8-14:20	Luke 20:27-47	Ps. 75:8-10
3-May	Judg. 15-16	Luke 21:1-19	Ps. 76:1-7
4-May	Judg. 17-18	Luke 21:20-22:6	Ps. 76:8-12
5-May	Judg. 19:1-20:23	Luke 22:7-30	Ps. 77:1-11
6-May	Judg. 20:24-21:25	Luke 22:31-54	Ps. 77:12-20
7-May	Ruth 1-2	Luke 22:55-23:25	Ps. 78:1-4
8-May	Ruth 3-4	Luke 23:26-24:12	Ps. 78:5-8
9-May	1 Sam. 1:1-2:21	Luke 24:13-53	Ps. 78:9-16
10-May	1 Sam. 2:22-4:22	John 1:1-28	Ps. 78:17-24
11-May	1 Sam. 5-7	John 1:29-51	Ps. 78:25-33
12-May	1 Sam. 8:1-9:26	John 2	Ps. 78:34-41
13-May	1 Sam. 9:27-11:15	John 3:1-22	Ps. 78:42-55
14-May	1 Sam. 12-13	John 3:23-4:10	Ps. 78:56-66
15-May	1 Sam. 14	John 4:11-38	Ps. 78:67-72
16-May	1 Sam. 15-16	John 4:39-54	Ps. 79:1-7
17-May	1 Sam. 17	John 5:1-24	Ps. 79:8-13
18-May	1 Sam. 18-19	John 5:25-47	Ps. 80:1-7
19-May	1 Sam. 20-21	John 6:1-21	Ps. 80:8-19
20-May	1 Sam. 22-23	John 6:22-42	Ps. 81:1-10
21-May	1 Sam. 24:1-25:31	John 6:43-71	Ps. 81:11-16
22-May	1 Sam. 25:32-27:12	John 7:1-24	Ps. 82
23-May	1 Sam. 28-29	John 7:25-8:11	Ps. 83
24-May	1 Sam. 30-31	John 8:12-47	Ps. 84:1-4

25-May	2 Sam. 1-2	John 8:48-9:12	Ps. 84:5-12
26-May	2 Sam. 3-4	John 9:13-34	Ps. 85:1-7
27-May	2 Sam. 5:1-7:17	John 9:35-10:10	Ps. 85:8-13
28-May	2 Sam. 7:18-10:19	John 10:11-30	Ps. 86:1-10
29-May	2 Sam. 11:1-12:25	John 10:31-11:16	Ps. 86:11-17
30-May	2 Sam. 12:26-13:39	John 11:17-54	Ps. 87
31-May	2 Sam. 14:1-15:12	John 11:55-12:19	Ps. 88:1-9
1-Jun	2 Sam. 15:13-16:23	John 12:20-43	Ps. 88:10-18
2-Jun	2 Sam. 17:1-18:18	John 12:44-13:20	Ps. 89:1-6
3-Jun	2 Sam. 18:19-19:39	John 13:21-38	Ps. 89:7-13
4-Jun	2 Sam. 19:40-21:22	John 14:1-17	Ps. 89:14-18
5-Jun	2 Sam. 22:1-23:7	John 14:18-15:27	Ps. 89:19-29
6-Jun	2 Sam. 23:8-24:25	John 16:1-22	Ps. 89:30-37
7-Jun	1 Kings 1	John 16:23-17:5	Ps. 89:38-52
8-Jun	1 Kings 2	John 17:6-26	Ps. 90:1-12
9-Jun	1 Kings 3-4	John 18:1-27	Ps. 90:13-17
10-Jun	1 Kings 5-6	John 18:28-19:5	Ps. 91:1-10
11-Jun	1 Kings 7	John 19:6-25a	Ps. 91:11-16
12-Jun	1 Kings 8:1-53	John 19:25b-42	Ps. 92:1-9
13-Jun	1 Kings 8:54-10:13	John 20:1-18	Ps. 92:10-15
14-Jun	1 Kings 10:14-11:43	John 20:19-31	Ps. 93
15-Jun	1 Kings 12:1-13:10	John 21	Ps. 94:1-11
16-Jun	1 Kings 13:11-14:31	Acts 1:1-11	Ps. 94:12-23
17-Jun	1 Kings 15:1-16:20	Acts 1:12-26	Ps. 95
18-Jun	1 Kings 16:21-18:19	Acts 2:1-21	Ps. 96:1-8
19-Jun	1 Kings 18:20-19:21	Acts 2:22-41	Ps. 96:9-13
20-Jun	1 Kings 20	Acts 2:42-3:26	Ps. 97:1-6
21-Jun	1 Kings 21:1-22:28	Acts 4:1-22	Ps. 97:7-12
22-Jun	1 Kings 22:29- 2 Kings 1:18	Acts 4:23-5:11	Ps. 98
23-Jun	2 Kings 2-3	Acts 5:12-28	Ps. 99
24-Jun	2 Kings 4	Acts 5:29-6:15	Ps. 100
25-Jun	2 Kings 5:1-6:23	Acts 7:1-16	Ps. 101
26-Jun	2 Kings 6:24-8:15	Acts 7:17-36	Ps. 102:1-7
27-Jun	2 Kings 8:16-9:37	Acts 7:37-53	Ps. 102:8-17
28-Jun	2 Kings 10-11	Acts 7:54-8:8	Ps. 102:18-28

29-Jun	2 Kings 12-13	Acts 8:9-40	Ps. 103:1-9
30-Jun	2 Kings 14-15	Acts 9:1-16	Ps. 103:10-14
1-Jul	2 Kings 16-17	Acts 9:17-31	Ps. 103:15-22
2-Jul	2 Kings 18:1-19:7	Acts 9:32-10:16	Ps. 104:1-9
3-Jul	2 Kings 19:8-20:21	Acts 10:17-33	Ps. 104:10-23
4-Jul	2 Kings 21:1-22:20	Acts 10:34-11:18	Ps. 104: 24-30
5-Jul	2 Kings 23	Acts 11:19-12:17	Ps. 104:31-35
6-Jul	2 Kings 24-25	Acts 12:18-13:13	Ps. 105:1-7
7-Jul	1 Chron. 1-2	Acts 13:14-43	Ps. 105:8-15
8-Jul	1 Chron. 3:1-5:10	Acts 13:44-14:10	Ps. 105:16-28
9-Jul	1 Chron. 5:11-6:81	Acts 14:11-28	Ps. 105:29-36
10-Jul	1 Chron. 7:1-9:9	Acts 15:1-18	Ps. 105:37-45
11-Jul	1 Chron. 9:10-11:9	Acts 15:19-41	Ps. 106:1-12
12-Jul	1 Chron. 11:10-12:40	Acts 16:1-15	Ps. 106:13-27
13-Jul	1 Chron. 13-15	Acts 16:16-40	Ps. 106:28-33
14-Jul	1 Chron. 16-17	Acts 17:1-14	Ps. 106:34-43
15-Jul	1 Chron. 18-20	Acts 17:15-34	Ps. 106:44-48
16-Jul	1 Chron. 21-22	Acts 18:1-23	Ps. 107:1-9
17-Jul	1 Chron. 23-25	Acts 18:24-19:10	Ps. 107:10-16
18-Jul	1 Chron. 26-27	Acts 19:11-22	Ps. 107:17-32
19-Jul	1 Chron. 28-29	Acts 19:23-41	Ps. 107:33-38
20-Jul	2 Chron. 1-3	Acts 20:1-16	Ps. 107:39-43
21-Jul	2 Chron. 4:1-6:11	Acts 20:17-38	Ps. 108
22-Jul	2 Chron. 6:12-7:10	Acts 21:1-14	Ps. 109:1-20
23-Jul	2 Chron. 7:11-9:28	Acts 21:15-32	Ps. 109:21-31
24-Jul	2 Chron. 9:29-12:16	Acts 21:33-22:16	Ps. 110:1-3
25-Jul	2 Chron. 13-15	Acts 22:17-23:11	Ps. 110:4-7
26-Jul	2 Chron. 16-17	Acts 23:12-24:21	Ps. 111
27-Jul	2 Chron. 18-19	Acts 24:22-25:12	Ps. 112
28-Jul	2 Chron. 20-21	Acts 25:13-27	Ps. 113
29-Jul	2 Chron. 22-23	Acts 26	Ps. 114
30-Jul	2 Chron. 24:1-25:16	Acts 27:1-20	Ps. 115:1-10
31-Jul	2 Chron. 25:17-27:9	Acts 27:21-28:6	Ps. 115:11-18
1-Aug	2 Chron. 28:1-29:19	Acts 28:7-31	Ps. 116:1-5
2-Aug	2 Chron. 29:20-30:27	Rom. 1:1-17	Ps. 116:6-19
3-Aug	2 Chron. 31-32	Rom. 1:18-32	Ps. 117

4-Aug	2 Chron. 33:1-34:7	Rom. 2	Ps. 118:1-18
5-Aug	2 Chron. 34:8-35:19	Rom. 3:1-26	Ps. 118:19-23
6-Aug	2 Chron. 35:20-36:23	Rom. 3:27-4:25	Ps. 118:24-29
7-Aug	Ezra 1-3	Rom. 5	Ps. 119:1-8
8-Aug	Ezra 4-5	Rom. 6:1-7:6	Ps. 119:9-16
9-Aug	Ezra 6:1-7:26	Rom. 7:7-25	Ps. 119:17-32
10-Aug	Ezra 7:27-9:4	Rom. 8:1-27	Ps. 119:33-40
11-Aug	Ezra 9:5-10:44	Rom. 8:28-39	Ps. 119:41-64
12-Aug	Neh. 1:1-3:16	Rom. 9:1-18	Ps. 119:65-72
13-Aug	Neh. 3:17-5:13	Rom. 9:19-33	Ps. 119:73-80
14-Aug	Neh. 5:14-7:73	Rom. 10:1-13	Ps. 119:81-88
15-Aug	Neh. 8:1-9:5	Rom. 10:14-11:24	Ps. 119:89-104
16-Aug	Neh. 9:6-10:27	Rom. 11:25-12:8	Ps. 119:105-120
17-Aug	Neh. 10:28-12:26	Rom. 12:9-13:7	Ps. 119:121-128
18-Aug	Neh. 12:27-13:31	Rom. 13:8-14:12	Ps. 119:129-136
19-Aug	Esther 1:1-2:18	Rom. 14:13-15:13	Ps. 119:137-152
20-Aug	Esther 2:19-5:14	Rom. 15:14-21	Ps. 119:153-168
21-Aug	Esther. 6-8	Rom. 15:22-33	Ps. 119:169-176
22-Aug	Esther 9-10	Rom. 16	Ps. 120-122
23-Aug	Job 1-3	1 Cor. 1:1-25	Ps. 123
24-Aug	Job 4-6	1 Cor. 1:26-2:16	Ps. 124-125
25-Aug	Job 7-9	1 Cor. 3	Ps. 126-127
26-Aug	Job 10-13	1 Cor. 4:1-13	Ps. 128-129
27-Aug	Job 14-16	1 Cor. 4:14-5:13	Ps. 130
28-Aug	Job 17-20	1 Cor. 6	Ps. 131
29-Aug	Job 21-23	1 Cor. 7:1-16	Ps. 132
30-Aug	Job 24-27	1 Cor. 7:17-40	Ps. 133-134
31-Aug	Job 28-30	1 Cor. 8	Ps. 135
1-Sep	Job 31-33	1 Cor. 9:1-18	Ps. 136:1-9
2-Sep	Job 34-36	1 Cor. 9:19-10:13	Ps. 136:10-26
3-Sep	Job 37-39	1 Cor. 10:14-11:1	Ps. 137
4-Sep	Job 40-42	1 Cor. 11:2-34	Ps. 138
5-Sep	Eccles. 1:1-3:15	1 Cor. 12:1-26	Ps. 139:1-6
6-Sep	Eccles. 3:16-6:12	1 Cor. 12:27-13:13	Ps. 139:7-18
7-Sep	Eccles. 7:1-9:12	1 Cor. 14:1-22	Ps. 139:19-24
8-Sep	Eccles. 9:13-12:14	1 Cor. 14:23-15:11	Ps. 140:1-8

9-Sep	SS 1-4	1 Cor. 15:12-34	Ps. 140:9-13
10-Sep	SS 5-8	1 Cor. 15:35-58	Ps. 141
11-Sep	Isa. 1-2	1 Cor. 16	Ps. 142
12-Sep	Isa. 3-5	2 Cor. 1:1-11	Ps. 143:1-6
13-Sep	Isa. 6-8	2 Cor. 1:12-2:4	Ps. 143:7-12
14-Sep	Isa. 9-10	2 Cor. 2:5-17	Ps. 144
15-Sep	Isa. 11-13	2 Cor. 3	Ps. 145
16-Sep	Isa. 14-16	2 Cor. 4	Ps. 146
17-Sep	Isa. 17-19	2 Cor. 5	Ps. 147:1-11
18-Sep	Isa. 20-23	2 Cor. 6	Ps. 147:12-20
19-Sep	Isa. 24:1-26:19	2 Cor. 7	Ps. 148
20-Sep	Isa. 26:20-28:29	2 Cor. 8	Ps. 149-150
21-Sep	Isa. 29-30	2 Cor. 9	Prov. 1:1-9
22-Sep	Isa. 31-33	2 Cor. 10	Prov. 1:10-22
23-Sep	Isa. 34-36	2 Cor. 11	Prov. 1:23-26
24-Sep	Isa. 37-38	2 Cor. 12:1-10	Prov. 1:27-33
25-Sep	Isa. 39-40	2 Cor. 12:11-13:14	Prov. 2:1-15
26-Sep	Isa. 41-42	Gal. 1	Prov. 2:16-22
27-Sep	Isa. 43:1-44:20	Gal. 2	Prov. 3:1-12
28-Sep	Isa. 44:21-46:13	Gal. 3:1-18	Prov. 3:13-26
29-Sep	Isa. 47:1-49:13	Gal 3:19-29	Prov. 3:27-35
30-Sep	Isa. 49:14-51:23	Gal 4:1-11	Prov. 4:1-19
1-Oct	Isa. 52-54	Gal. 4:12-31	Prov. 4:20-27
2-Oct	Isa. 55-57	Gal. 5	Prov. 5:1-14
3-Oct	Isa. 58-59	Gal. 6	Prov. 5:15-23
4-Oct	Isa. 60-62	Eph. 1	Prov. 6:1-5
5-Oct	Isa. 63:1-65:16	Eph. 2	Prov. 6:6-19
6-Oct	Isa. 65:17-66:24	Eph. 3:1-4:16	Prov. 6:20-26
7-Oct	Jer. 1-2	Eph. 4:17-32	Prov. 6:27-35
8-Oct	Jer. 3:1-4:22	Eph. 5	Prov. 7:1-5
9-Oct	Jer. 4:23-5:31	Eph. 6	Prov. 7:6-27
10-Oct	Jer. 6:1-7:26	Phil. 1:1-26	Prov. 8:1-11
11-Oct	Jer. 7:26-9:16	Phil. 1:27-2:18	Prov. 8:12-21
12-Oct	Jer. 9:17-11:17	Phil 2:19-30	Prov. 8:22-36
13-Oct	Jer. 11:18-13:27	Phil. 3	Prov. 9:1-6
14-Oct	Jer. 14-15	Phil. 4	Prov. 9:7-18

15-Oct	Jer. 16-17	Col. 1:1-23	Prov. 10:1-5
16-Oct	Jer. 18:1-20:6	Col. 1:24-2:15	Prov. 10:6-14
17-Oct	Jer. 20:7-22:19	Col. 2:16-3:4	Prov. 10:15-26
18-Oct	Jer. 22:20-23:40	Col. 3:5-4:1	Prov. 10:27-32
19-Oct	Jer. 24-25	Col. 4:2-18	Prov. 11:1-11
20-Oct	Jer. 26-27	1 Thes. 1:1-2:8	Prov. 11:12-21
21-Oct	Jer. 28-29	1 Thes. 2:9-3:13	Prov. 11:22-26
22-Oct	Jer. 30:1-31:22	1 Thes. 4:1-5:11	Prov. 11:27-31
23-Oct	Jer. 31:23-32:35	1 Thes. 5:12-28	Prov. 12:1-14
24-Oct	Jer. 32:36-34:7	2 Thes. 1-2	Prov. 12:15-20
25-Oct	Jer. 34:8-36:10	2 Thes. 3	Prov. 12:21-28
26-Oct	Jer. 36:11-38:13	1 Tim. 1:1-17	Prov. 13:1-4
27-Oct	Jer. 38:14-40:6	1 Tim. 1:18-3:13	Prov. 13:5-13
28-Oct	Jer. 40:7-42:22	1 Tim. 3:14-4:10	Prov. 13:14-21
29-Oct	Jer. 43-44	1 Tim. 4:11-5:16	Prov. 13:22-25
30-Oct	Jer. 45-47	1 Tim. 5:17-6:21	Prov. 14:1-6
31-Oct	Jer. 48:1-49:6	2 Tim. 1	Prov. 14:7-22
1-Nov	Jer. 49:7-50:16	2 Tim. 2	Prov. 14:23-27
2-Nov	Jer. 50:17-51:14	2 Tim. 3	Prov. 14:28-35
3-Nov	Jer. 51:15-64	2 Tim. 4	Prov. 15:1-9
4-Nov	Jer. 52-Lam. 1	Ti. 1:1-9	Prov. 15:10-17
5-Nov	Lam. 2:1-3:38	Ti. 1:10-2:15	Prov. 15:18-26
6-Nov	Lam. 3:39-5:22	Ti. 3	Prov. 15:27-33
7-Nov	Ezek. 1:1-3:21	Philemon 1	Prov. 16:1-9
8-Nov	Ezek. 3:22-5:17	Heb. 1:1-2:4	Prov. 16:10-21
9-Nov	Ezek. 6-7	Heb. 2:5-18	Prov. 16:22-33
10-Nov	Ezek. 8-10	Heb. 3:1-4:3	Prov. 17:1-5
11-Nov	Ezek. 11-12	Heb. 4:4-5:10	Prov. 17:6-12
12-Nov	Ezek. 13-14	Heb. 5:11-6:20	Prov. 17:13-22
13-Nov	Ezek. 15:1-16:43	Heb. 7:1-28	Prov. 17:23-28
14-Nov	Ezek. 16:44-17:24	Heb. 8:1-9:10	Prov. 18:1-7
15-Nov	Ezek. 18-19	Heb. 9:11-28	Prov. 18:8-17
16-Nov	Ezek. 20	Heb. 10:1-25	Prov. 18:18-24
17-Nov	Ezek. 21-22	Heb. 10:26-39	Prov. 19:1-8
18-Nov	Ezek. 23	Heb. 11:1-31	Prov. 19:9-14
19-Nov	Ezek. 24-26	Heb. 11:32-40	Prov. 19:15-21

20-Nov	Ezek. 27-28	Heb. 12:1-13	Prov. 19:22-29
21-Nov	Ezek. 29-30	Heb. 12:14-29	Prov. 20:1-18
22-Nov	Ezek. 31-32	Heb. 13	Prov. 20:19-24
23-Nov	Ezek. 33:1-34:10	Jas. 1	Prov. 20:25-30
24-Nov	Ezek. 34:11-36:15	Jas. 2	Prov. 21:1-8
25-Nov	Ezek. 36:16-37:28	Jas. 3	Prov. 21:9-18
26-Nov	Ezek. 38-39	Jas. 4:1-5:6	Prov. 21:19-24
27-Nov	Ezek. 40	Jas. 5:7-20	Prov. 21:25-31
28-Nov	Ezek. 41:1-43:12	1 Pet. 1:1-12	Prov. 22:1-9
29-Nov	Ezek. 43:13-44:31	1 Pet. 1:13-2:3	Prov. 22:10-23
30-Nov	Ezek. 45-46	1 Pet. 2:4-17	Prov. 22:24-29
1-Dec	Ezek. 47-48	1 Pet. 2:18-3:7	Prov. 23:1-9
2-Dec	Dan. 1:1-2:23	1 Pet. 3:8-4:19	Prov. 23:10-16
3-Dec	Dan. 2:24-3:30	1 Pet. 5	Prov. 23:17-25
4-Dec	Dan. 4	2 Pet. 1	Prov. 23:26-35
5-Dec	Dan. 5	2 Pet. 2	Prov. 24:1-18
6-Dec	Dan. 6:1-7:14	2 Pet. 3	Prov. 24:19-27
7-Dec	Dan. 7:15-8:27	1 John 1:1-2:17	Prov. 24:28-34
8-Dec	Dan. 9-10	1 John 2:18-29	Prov. 25:1-12
9-Dec	Dan. 11-12	1 John 3:1-12	Prov. 25:13-17
10-Dec	Hos. 1-3	1 John 3:13-4:16	Prov. 25:18-28
11-Dec	Hos. 4-6	1 John 4:17-5:21	Prov. 26:1-16
12-Dec	Hos. 7-10	2 John	Prov. 26:17-21
13-Dec	Hos. 11-14	3 John	Prov. 26:22-27:9
14-Dec	Joel 1:1-2:17	Jude	Prov. 27:10-17
15-Dec	Joel 2:18-3:21	Rev. 1:1-2:11	Prov. 27:18-27
16-Dec	Amos 1:1-4:5	Rev. 2:12-29	Prov. 28:1-8
17-Dec	Amos 4:6-6:14	Rev. 3	Prov. 28:9-16
18-Dec	Amos 7-9	Rev. 4:1-5:5	Prov. 28:17-24
19-Dec	Obad-Jonah	Rev. 5:6-14	Prov. 28:25-28
20-Dec	Mic. 1:1-4:5	Rev. 6:1-7:8	Prov. 29:1-8
21-Dec	Mic. 4:6-7:20	Rev. 7:9-8:13	Prov. 29:9-14
22-Dec	Nah. 1-3	Rev. 9-10	Prov. 29:15-23
23-Dec	Hab. 1-3	Rev. 11	Prov. 29:24-27
24-Dec	Zeph. 1-3	Rev. 12	Prov. 30:1-6
25-Dec	Hag. 1-2	Rev. 13:1-14:13	Prov. 30:7-16

26-Dec	Zech. 1-4	Rev. 14:14-16:3	Prov. 30:17-20
27-Dec	Zech. 5-8	Rev. 16:4-21	Prov. 30:21-28
28-Dec	Zech. 9-11	Rev. 17:1-18:8	Prov. 30:29-33
29-Dec	Zech. 12-14	Rev. 18:9-24	Prov. 31:1-9
30-Dec	Mal. 1-2	Rev. 19-20	Prov. 31:10-17
31-Dec	Mal. 3-4	Rev. 21-22	Prov. 31:18-31